I0464115

LEADING *with* NOBILITY *and* HONOUR

Leadership with Principle and Values

MAURICE COLLIS

ISBN: 978-1-4834-8416-7 (sc)
ISBN: 978-1-4834-8415-0 (e)

Lulu Publishing Services rev. date: 04/19/2018

CONTENTS

This book is dedicated to my wife, Lidia, who always encourages me to write. If I do have any inspiration I draw it from her.

It is also for my children: Marie, Michael, Victoria, William and Julia.

My thanks are given to Nada Genadry, Human Resources Director, Libanpost who kindly provided the foreword

Foreword from Nada Genadry, Human Resources Director, Libanpost

In his book, Maurice Collis – an experienced HR practitioner - bravely tackles an important organizational topic: toxic behavior at work and how it impacts colleagues' relations, authority, and undermines organizational performance. He draws on real cases he encountered during his long years of practice; cases that many of us will be able to relate to, as they are unfortunately far too common in our organizations. Each chapter of the book presents a situation and the interactions that took place, and ends with a key learning drawn from the Charlemagne's code of chivalry for knights. A code of nobility.

The book title "Leading with nobility and honour" may sound at first as a completely outdated concept drawn from another era... But is it really? In the dictionary, nobility refers to the "quality of being noble in character". Its synonyms encompass qualities such as virtue, goodness, honor, honesty, decency, integrity, magnanimity, generosity, selflessness and bravery, which, if we think of them for a minute, are not only medieval concepts...

So why the need for such a book now? Financial scandals that put at risk the global economy through systemic effects shake the planet every now and then, burnouts and other sad events such as employee suicides keep on ringing the bell. Why should we allow ourselves to reach such levels? Maurice rightfully claims that if bad behaviors persist in companies, it is because they are not faced with proper consequences. Add to that the fact that, what is considered as inappropriate differs sometimes drastically from one person to the next, and we have a recipe for the propagation of wrongdoing and the spreading of unhealthy organizational cultures.

A book such as this one has the merit of describing real practices and of recommending constructive alternatives at work. Indeed, codes of conduct do exist in companies but they usually cover topics such as dress code, non-religious nonpolitical talking, harassment, conflict of interests, confidentiality, non-compete, etc. It is not common to encounter a business code of conduct, or a business ethics course for that matter, that tackles decent behavior among colleagues. This is particularly important as organizations are economic and social constructs, where human beings spend a large part of their time. In the best cases, companies may represent spaces of self-actualization and shared success, while in some cases they are more like arenas where jungle like behaviors of "survival of the fittest" are widespread and where "the end justifies the means".

As a specialist of human and social nature with a solid business acumen, Maurice describes what may contribute to safeguard organizations and people alike from undue abuses. The principles that the reader will uncover throughout the book may sound like common sense. Indeed, they are simple to understand but so important to promote and even enforce at times.

Being in charge of others, facing important responsibilities, concluding big deals, all require - on top of a set of qualifications and skills -, a strong character to be ready to face temptation, resist stress and lead others with care. The ancients knew it. Their rituals were designed to shed light on important moments of crossings. As an example, prior to being put in charge of others, one had to go through an initiating ceremony of a 10 hour long vigil before knighthood; a sort of inner contemplation to get ready for the role.

In the past, religious, school and family education took a role in shaping character. Less so now, except where extremism leads to dangerous excesses… Companies have to do their share. However, too often still, attention is only focused on technical and managerial skills, as well as on demonstrated performance. In a few fortunate workplaces, attitude has become key, as all the rest can be taught. This book may be used as a tool for companies' trainers, for university and school educational programs, in order to foster healthier environments and a better togetherness, until such values become again an intrinsic part of our personal and professional identities. Isn't it said that "Integrity asks not what others think about you but what you think about yourself?"

With his book "Leading with nobility and honor", Maurice Collis revives the little voice within.

Nada Génadry

12 December 2016

Foreword from Maurice Collis

This book has been in the writing for the last few years. The idea formed when coming across a reference to Charlemagne's code of Chivalry for knights. As a youngster, like many, I became fascinated with the world of King Arthur and the Knights of the Round Table. I was introduced to some of the concepts of honour and nobility which these days are words that we do not often see in print.

Over the recent years there has been a succession of acts arising from executives in large companies which would not conform to any code of honour or conduct. In some cases, following ignominious acts individuals will profit from the wrong doings through a book and film deal and make headlines all for the wrong reasons. And yet those very acts have affected the lives of people around them and in major cases rippled outwards into a wider community.

In my view, this all stems from the fact that wrong doing is no longer accompanied with a sense of shame. A shrug of the shoulders and "moving on" seems to be all that it takes when an individual is discovered to have acted and behaved in ways that affect businesses and the lives of people. And indeed there are very few occasions when the community shuns the wrong doer for such behaviour, although this is now changing significantly.

Just before I commenced writing this book, I spent a weekend reviewing business articles and came across a comment in an article where the author – a senior manager - stated that 'of course what doesn't get rewarded does not get done'. Although this is not a new statement it always seems to go unchallenged. Is it true now that nobody will do anything unless there is a buck on the end of it? I don't think so. There are many who are intrinsically motivated and carry out their work for many reasons, not least because they wish to gain mastery in their field of choice. However, I do believe that when they have leaders with the right principles and values that they can do so much more.

However in the absence of such a leader and a noble cause, then yes it is possible that for many the transaction will simply become a service in exchange for money.

Reading through the articles that weekend I was, and not for the first time, struck by how much real leadership is needed and the desire to find a way for employees to engage with the objectives of the company. Gareth Jones and Rob Goffee aptly sum it all up in their seminal work of a few years back:

Why should anyone be led by you?

It is true that acquiring knowledge and job skills from their seniors is essential for employees wishing to learn from their leaders. But there is so much more to it. Of course good leaders and managers normally have knowledge and job skill in buckets. However, as well as this, most employees also want a leader who they can admire and respect. And so my argument is that it is a necessity for the leader to have a noble character, to be honourable and to have an element of gravitas. That is not to say they cannot be humorous. In fact they should but in all they do they should generate feelings of trust and respect.

Where it all goes wrong is when a leader's actions destroy the belief in nobility and hence the leader falls from grace. There are many reasons why this might arise but there is no real universal code in place by which those who are in positions of authority may be judged for wrongdoing. This is left to the courts to deal with.

It is true that there are some professions, such as the legal and medical, which can disbar individuals for wrong practicing for a variety of reasons. Directors in companies may also be disbarred but these are primarily financially related.

There is a need for a more robust code of conduct which is universally accepted and which has the power to discipline and punish executives for infractions of that code. Without this, in my view, we will continue to see a lack of character, integrity and yes, nobility, amongst those we wish to admire.

The chapters which follow this introduction deal with a series of incidents in a short story format which are typical in many organisations and companies but which may well go unnoticed. The company is a fictional nation wide chain of stores and the story is told by a lifelong senior member of the company, David Adams who is the Organisation Development Director. You may well recognize some of the incidents and this is because they are based on commonplace occurrences in organisations and not on any specific incident.

Maurice Collis

26 December 2016

CHARLEMAGNE CODE OF CHIVALRY

The Charlemagne Code of chivalry was well known in its time and the knights revered the code and followed it. If you have never seen it before I have reproduced it below.

- To fear God and maintain his church
- To serve the liege lord in valour and faith
- To protect the weak and defenceless
- To give succour to widows and orphans
- To refrain from the wanton giving of offence
- To live by honour and for glory
- To despise pecuniary reward
- To fight for the welfare of all
- To obey those placed in authority
- To guard the honour of fellow knights
- To eschew unfairness, meanness and deceit
- At all times to speak the truth
- To persevere to the end in any enterprise begun
- To respect the honour of women
- Never to refuse a challenge from an equal
- Never to turn the back upon a foe

CODE OF HONOUR – MODERN DAY

In many respects the Charlemagne chivalric code may not be exactly suitable for the present day. What I have done is to update it into a modern day Code of Honour for Managers and Leaders – and why not all of us – to follow. This modern day code of honour has followed the principles of the Charlemagne Code of Chivalry as far as it can and brought up to date for the challenges of modern day business life. The principles of the Code of Honour are produced below:

Principle 1: The lawful instructions of your Manager must be followed.

When the Manager has come to a decision and discussed it with the team, the team has a right to make an objection but they do not have the right to overrule it. Any individual who finds that they are not comfortable with the decision because it conflicts with a fundamental principle of their own should transfer or resign. It is not correct to stay and seek to undermine the decision or the position of their Manager.

Principle 2: All Managers must observe a code of practice that sets out principles and values and which must always be observed.

The Manager must have a known set of principles and values and abide by them. They cannot be set aside once adopted. Once a Manager has become a Manager he or she must commit to the principles in writing and accept the consequences of peers and seniors if they are abandoned.

Principle 3: Defend individuals in junior positions who are unfairly or harshly treated by those with power.

A leader has a duty to defend his or her team and anyone junior who may be suffering from harsh and unnecessary treatment from those who have greater power.

Principle 4: Provide personal and financial help to a family, group or local charitable cause for which you have an affinity. It should be with

personal involvement and not remote financial help and should not be publicized. It is a selfless act.

All Managers should find a charitable act outside the workplace to help others. It does not necessarily need to be financial aid. It can be selfless assistance that will help others with no expectation of anything to be received in return.

Principle 5. No Manager should ever give offence to any person within or outside the organization. Personal attacks based on different personality, race, religion, physical appearance etc are not to be tolerated.

We are all required to work across multicultural and diverse groups. Association with others is based on respect and mutual trust and we should never knowingly harm or hurt others through word or deed.

Principle 6: A positive attitude, determination and self belief is essential in ensuring that a Manager can work with a team to fulfill objectives.

We cannot enter into any activity without positivity, energy and enthusiasm that we use to inspire our teams. If we cannot do this we should choose not to lead people.

Principle 7: Value achievement and the development of others more than personal reward.

Every manager needs to earn financial reward to exist but it cannot be the only reason. All managers must develop others and focus on achieving results for the organization that they serve.

Principle 8: Ensure credit and reward is fairly shared with all the team.

It is the duty of leaders to develop others and encourage ideas. The ideas should not be stolen and a good leader ensures credit is given to and publicly acknowledges the originator of the idea.

Principle 9: Support and follow the instructions of your boss

As leaders we can and should make our point of view known and argue our case strongly. This is what makes for better decisions but once that decision is made the arguments are over and we move to implementation. No-one has the right to undermine and sabotage a senior's lawful instruction.

Principle 10: Support your Peers

There is no competition with peers. Leaders must know that we are all one team and that internal conflicts and lack of support lead to lack of focus on the customer, whether they are external or internal.

Principle 11: Resist meanness, unfairness and deceit

No leader should ever take decisions that are intended to embarrass or punish another unfairly. Power over others needs to be exercised lightly and with absolute transparency. Doing otherwise is a flagrant abuse of that power.

Principle 12: Persevere to the end in any enterprise begun

No strategy is easy and sometimes it can seem easy to stop and try something else. However, unless it is clear that the strategy is a disaster all leaders should be determined and remain focused on completing what has been started.

Principle 13: Respect the dignity of others and not abuse position

Leaders should never use their power to obtain favours from subordinates or others for any reason whatsoever. The dignity of juniors should always be maintained.

Principle 14: Never backdown when an unfair challenge is made by a peer

Regrettably competition can find its way into peer to peer relations as some strive for recognition from the senior management team and to assume a position of superiority over their peers. This can take the form of an attack on others and leaders should never back away from an aggressive and unfair challenge.

Principle 15: A good leader always shows courage and determination in the face of difficulty

Courage is an essential feature of leadership. A lack of it may often mean that individuals will choose a weaker course of action that will not benefit the organization or company.

Principle 16 – A leader always tells the truth without evasion

The truth about a situation is the only way for a leader to speak and behave. Any other route is not the principle of a leader and creates further complexities at a later stage

Foreword: Leading with Nobility and Honour

In the chapters that follow we will meet David Adams who considers incidents that have arisen during his lifetime and which have either exemplified the principles of the Code and show how individuals have been found to be acting with honour and nobility or not.

This book is written in story form.

CHAPTER 1

I woke at the usual time but stayed in bed and lay there thinking, with eyes open and focused on the ceiling. It did not feel like the best period of my life. Fifteen minutes later, Diane's alarm sounded and she woke from her sleep. As her eyes focused I could see that she was curious as to why I had not risen to take a shower earlier.

"David, did you oversleep?" She asked with curiosity in her voice.

"No, I didn't." I paused and then said, "I'm not going in to the office today."

"Are you ill?" Diane asked reaching out to touch him with concern.

"No, I'm not ill. Just tired. I don't feel like going in today."

Diane rose up on her elbow to look at me. "You don't feel like going in? I've never heard you say that in the twenty two years of our marriage."

"Yup," I said. "Today is a first."

"Are you sure you're ok? She asked reaching out to touch his forehead.

"Yes, I'm ok, Diane. I just want to rest and think things through."

She sat up sharply.

"Has something happened David. Something I should know about."

I turned to look at my wife of so many years. I could see a little fear and maybe suspicion in her eyes. Although why this should be I did not know.

I reached out for her hand and looked into her eyes. "No there's nothing, Diane". I smiled warmly and affectionately. "I'm just tired and need to think, that's all."

She relaxed visibly and nodded. "I'll take my shower then."

Later my children, Tom and Sara, came to the bedroom before they left for school. They too had curiosity in their eyes.

"You getting executive burn out, Dad?" Tom asked with half a smile on his face.

"Maybe you should see a doctor, Dad," Sara said more worried than her brother.

"I'm fine!" I said with a laugh. "Now get off to school and let me rest."

Once she was ready for work Diane came to check on me again and then left with the children. Once they had left the house I relaxed into the bed. This was it, I thought, "I've had enough. I just do not enjoy my working life anymore and the way people behave at work." No matter which way I look at it something has to change but I just cannot say what this should be.

To be honest I knew that I was in some kind of malaise, perhaps even a slight depression. I wondered if this was now my very own mid life crisis. Well, I mused, I am 46 years old after all. I even managed a smile.

I decided to look back over my life. To all intents and purposes it had not been a bad one. I had originated from a middle class background living in a good neighbourhood. My father taught history at a local high school and my mother was an accountant. They were both retired now and I visited them regularly. My older brother was an officer in the Army and still is, and my younger sister developed a good business making dresses for wealthy and discerning clients who wanted the designer look without the designer prices.

As a boy I looked up to my older brother. He was older by two years and was a legend at school – superb at study and at sport: the winning combination. He was – and still is, – athletically built and imposing. He was and is afraid of no-one.

He had always given me great advice at school:

Don't lie
Don't cheat
Work as hard as you can
Play as hard as you want
Be Friendly
Don't bully others and don't be bullied.

I was scared the day I went to High School as I walked along with my brother.

"Ed, I'm a bit scared", I said to him resisting the urge to grab his hand.

Ed laughed. "So was I on the first day. We all are."

"What. You...were scared?" I asked in amazement.

"Yes of course. The trick is not show it, that's all. And that's what you've got to do. Looking nervous attracts trouble."

"But I've got you anyway........" I looked at Ed and my voice trailed away. The look on his face was enough and I knew he was right. I could never hide behind my brother. Although it was tempting, it would not be possible. I could see that.

"Dave, you've been to Judo club with me since you were seven years old. You're good. If anyone goes for you use your skill. Keep breathing, stay light on your feet, wait for the move and deal with it. Don't back off."

His advice was always good, I thought. I followed it and although I was never the most assertive in my school years my look of defiance against intimidation was enough to put off most bullies. I missed Ed so much when he left the school for Sandhurst but, although the Army claimed my brother, I always looked forward to our meetings and discussions.

I remembered particularly one discussion after Ed's passing out parade at Sandhurst. My brother looked magnificent during that occasion. He did not seem proud or aggressive, rather confident and calm.

During the celebration I asked him, and not for the first time, why he wanted to be an Army Officer. In the past, my brother had evaded this question merely saying that it was for him a vocation. This time he was more specific.

"Why did I choose the Army?" He smiled. "I'll tell you. There is a code of honour if you like which I don't see anywhere else. In other professions nobody has to live up to any standards. It's easy to self delude and slip into a sleazy code of behaviour just because that's the norm. Nobility in it's truest sense is a word that you never hear anymore because very few live up to it or want to live up to it. Our society doesn't want it and in fact smirks at it as an outmoded and unnecessary concept."

I shifted in my bed. My brother had seen it then all those years ago, I mused. He was always so much more insightful than me.

Inspired by my brother I lived my own code of honour at school and at home. I did not cheat at homework or exams although I had seen others do so and seen their marks edge past my own because of this sometimes – but neither did I blow the whistle on them.

I knew also that I was no genius at schoolwork. There were others who learned with ease. It was not that easy for me but I discovered that reasonable intelligence coupled with the willingness to set aside time and work hard made up for innate intelligence.

I even began to believe that the brain was a muscle and the more you practiced the smarter it became! I might not have got there as fast as some of the others but I got there and often found I was able to go further than the brighter ones who were not prepared to put in the effort. It was just a question of determination and hard work. My name did not appear in the lists of those who won special awards for subjects, and I never found myself amongst the first three students in the class. I was a little above average and in being so was not high enough to attract the attention and admiration of others and not low enough to attract the displeasure of the school powers or the adulation of students who admired a rebel.

I didn't bully anyone and I was not bullied. I reflected that this for many years was more because of my brother's powerful presence rather than anything else. However, when a bully's eyes wandered in my direction I met them clearly and directly just as my brother advised. Nobody bothered to find out if my confident gaze was a bluff.

I played sports at school – cricket and rugby – and was good enough to make the school first teams but I was not a brilliant player. I was occasionally ridiculed by some of my teammates because of the position I took on decisions. I always walked if I knew I had nicked the ball and it was taken cleanly by the 'keeper without waiting for the umpire's decision. Some of my teammates thought this did not show support for the team. I would say that if we were to win it would have to be a fair win, otherwise it would not be a clean win. Sometimes they looked at me as if I was crazy.

I have always been involved with a group of friends at school but I often felt that I was in the group but not part of the group. We went to football, rugby and cricket games as a group. We also socialized together – at parties and cinemas and as we got older at pubs and clubs. But when things got out of hand and involved minor damage, rowdy behaviour and intimidation – as it sometimes did – I found that if I did join in it was without enthusiasm and afterwards always left me with guilt. I just preferred not to behave badly and that was it.

My attitude in this regard was more obvious in my last year at school. "You don't like breaking the rules do you, Dave?" one said to me with a smile, a smile full of curiosity but also disbelief and indeed some mocking.

"Why do you ask?" I couldn't help feeling suspicious. Maybe my friend was looking for an opportunity to ridicule.

My questioner shrugged his shoulders. "Just curious, that's all."

I pondered before answering. I didn't want to set myself up for weeks of sarcastic remarks. "Most rules make sense," I replied. "Breaking them usually means that someone else suffers although you might not realize it at first."

"But breaking rules is fun!" my friend shot back.

"Is it?" I responded equally as quickly. "I'm not sure about that. I can't help feeling uncomfortable or guilty. But it's not just about breaking rules either, is it? It's about doing the right thing and deep down we all know what the right thing is."

"But it doesn't matter if nobody finds out, does it?"

"It does for me," I responded. "Maybe it should for you too. Remember, it is easier to do the wrong thing if nobody else cares and you follow the crowd. It's hard sometimes to do the right thing. It's easy to follow a crowd and fit in."

"Hey look, Serpico," he said and I could see that I had gone too far. "Your way is not for me. It's too much like goody two shoes. Without a few thrills it's only a half life. I'll opt for the thrills."

"There's thrills without breaking rules, isn't there," I replied with a smile. "But look, I don't ask anyone to share my view on this. I keep it to myself.

And as you know I take part in what we do but sometimes I have regrets about it. As you say, I don't like breaking the rules but sometimes I do.' After his friend left I mulled things over. I wondered if my position made other people feel uncomfortable. It crossed my mind that not joining in – or not appearing to enjoy yourself when joining in – causes problems for the others.

And thus it was throughout my school and University career. I found some like-minded individuals wherever I was but it seemed to me and to most of those with whom I associated with, that acting with honour and a degree of nobility was a relic of the past. It was simply fine to cheat, copy work, take credit where it was not due, speak badly of others behind their backs and a whole host of other things. And all this simply because everyone else did it. But that did not make it right, only convenient to behave that way.

When I left university I joined a major retailer as a graduate trainee and I built my career within the group over a period of twenty two years. In the early years I learned many of the departmental functions and worked in stores in varying roles. In the more recent years I moved towards Organisational Development and three years previously I became Head of the OD Department reporting to the main Board HR Director.

The role suited me and my beliefs but over the years I found that I accepted the bad behaviours that I saw around me. Often I asked myself the question if they really were bad behaviours. Perhaps I argued to myself, unconvincingly, that it was my unique way of looking at things.

As a child it was easier to walk away from things that were uncomfortable to me and therefore feel that I was not involved. As an adult it was not possible to walk away. In the organization I worked for, there were times when I felt horrified at what I had seen. But I did not leave; I did not resign and I did not complain to anyone. Maybe in a half-hearted way I pointed out that certain things were perhaps not acceptable or appropriate. However, in most cases, unless issues were a disciplinary offence in the gross misconduct category most people seemed to turn a blind eye. And so had I, I mused. In doing so, I knew within myself, that in so doing I tacitly "approved" the behaviours.

I realized that most misdoings did in fact arise in that shadowy area where those involved knew deep down that their actions may not be morally, ethically or humanly right. But it mattered less and less as each ignoble act was carried out. Maybe some people felt some vague discomfort or a feeling that it should not really be this way. If this happened either they were not in a sufficient position of power to do anything about it or there was risk of social exclusion if they did suggest that there was something wrong. It was only the really brave and principled who could walk alone and be akin to "whistle-blowers". It often happened too that those who acted ignobly were those most respected by the organization for other skills – sales, management skills, problem solving, innovation, strategy, negotiation and a host of other activities.

I sighed! "The world is too much with us, late and soon" I mused. I swung my legs out of bed and decided that a shower and no shave were the precursors to further thought.

After I showered and dressed casually I picked up my pocket items from the bedside table and my mobile phone. Walking downstairs, the mobile rang.

"Are you up now?" Diane asked cheerily. "Or still moping in bed."

"Moping in bed, of course," I felt better and was in the mood for some light-hearted banter.

"Are you sure?' she asked. "I can smell coffee."

I smiled. She had heard me start the coffee percolator after walking into the kitchen

"Nothing gets past you, does it?" I joked. "I often wonder if I'm on camera!!"

"Smile please", she chuckled and then more seriously. "So what are your plans today?

"I thought I'd drive over to the beach chalet, have a think and then take lunch at the Swan about one pm or so. Why don't you come over?"

I held my breath. I knew that it would be difficult for Diane to get away. I sensed that she was weighing up the obligations to work and to me. I hoped the balance would tip in my favour.

The pause may just have been a matter of seconds but I knew that it contained a lot of mental thought. "Sounds a great idea," she said. "Just what we both need. I'll be at the Swan around one. If you have your first glass of red wine without me I'll try not to be too jealous."

"Thanks Diane," I said softly and with feeling. I knew that her choice to leave was not easy, but there was no-one whose company I enjoyed more than that of my wife.

The drive to their chalet did not take more than 30 minutes. I smiled to myself: a chalet did sound grand. In reality the chalet was a wooden cabin with just a few rooms (living area with kitchen, two bedrooms) and a bathroom. There were twenty or so such "chalets" in a line on a piece of grass land with stone pathways to each chalet. They overlooked the sandy beach that was 100 metres away.

In the summer time when school holidays were in full swing, the beach would have many families all across the area but in May there were just a few couples (wearing warm jackets) making their way across the long beach. It was only 10.30 am and I knew that there might be more families arriving later as the day warmed up.

I opened the door to the chalet and found what I was looking for on a shelf in the living area. It was a Moleskine note book that I purchased out of curiosity after reading Bruce Chatwin's "Songlines". I do not regard myself as an author but the idea of purchasing a notebook in which you jotted your musings appealed to me. Then why had I placed it here at the chalet, I thought to myself? Do I only really think, when I'm here? It was an interesting question.

A small voice from within my mind suggested that I might only really think when I wasn't at work. Had I read somewhere years back that efficiency and creativity were opposites? Did the process of work make you more efficient, I wondered, and less creative?

I searched the bookshelf for an article I had researched on the internet some months back. I found it. It was "Charlemagne's Code of Chivalry" which the medieval knight lived by. I found that the code they lived by had meaning for me and some relevance even in the modern day world. I read through the code once again to remind myself of the principles:

- To fear God and maintain his church
- To serve the liege lord in valour and faith
- To protect the weak and defenceless
- To give succour to widows and orphans
- To refrain from the wanton giving of offence
- To live by honour and for glory
- To despise pecuniary reward
- To fight for the welfare of all
- To obey those placed in authority
- To guard the honour of fellow knights
- To eschew unfairness, meanness and deceit
- At all times to speak the truth
- To persevere to the end in any enterprise begun
- To respect the honour of women
- Never to refuse a challenge from an equal
- Never to turn the back upon a foe

I felt there was something here that could be developed as a code of principles for working life. As things stood, nobody had any ethically meaningful measures by which to be judged. Measures were primarily bottom line related.

In mulling things over, I felt the warmth of the sun grow stronger and the urge to find a pen and sit out on the wooden verandah to get to work became irresistible. I found one and closed the door behind me and sat down on the wooden bench. It was shaped and contoured and reasonably comfortable but I guessed I would need that cushion later.

Before opening the notebook I looked out again across the beach and the sea. The wash of the surf hitting the sand came as a soft hiss up to me. This gentle sound, the warmth of the sun and the peacefulness of this place allowed me to relax. I felt a burden slip from my shoulders as I breathed in the oxygen-rich air spiced with tangy salt from the sea.

I opened the notebook. There were one or two jottings from before. Mostly they were quotations I'd found while reading or musings about situations and problems at my office. I turned to the first blank page and stared at it.

Then I wrote in capital letters – FINDING NOBILITY.

That was the easy part I thought to myself but to where did the title lead? I looked out across the beach and sea again, watching a young woman throw a small ball into the sea for her black Labrador to retrieve. The dog came close to her full of seawater and I watched as the dog shook himself so that spray flew from his fur in every direction. The young woman retreated fearful of a soaking and the dog was oblivious to her concern.

The image gave me the inspiration I was looking for. I needed first to look at those who wittingly or unwittingly had "showered" others. That shouldn't be difficult, I smiled to myself.

My mind went back to Janet Ainsley.

CHAPTER 2

Janet Ainsley

Janet Ainsley happened to be one of my first Managers at the Company. She was the Personnel Manager at one of the largest stores in Birmingham. Janet was a divorcee of around 38 years of age, a petite blonde, sharply intelligent and with a pretty face and exquisite figure. She really looked as if butter would melt in her mouth and she was certainly aware she could melt the hearts of most around her – including mine, I mused.

She was fearfully protecting of her own team but also champion for any employee she considered was being treated badly or unfairly by other managers. Her definition of fairness did, however, seem to lean heavily towards the employee.

I remembered that in one discussion with her I had ventured to say. "They are not all angels, you know, Janet. Some of them do seem to need a damn good reprimand."

I had seen the look before used on others but this time it was brought to bear on me. It altered her entire features. Gone was the petite blonde with a sugary smile and in her place I found I was staring straight at the wicked witch of the north. She unleashed the withering look full of contempt, scorn and pity and I had to break eye contact. It made me smile now but I remembered how uncomfortable it had been years ago. The look was so all-embracing it did not need words to convey any meaning. I mumbled that there was somebody I needed to speak to in another Department.

There was no doubt in my mind that in most respects Janet was a superb manager but as events unfolded I realized that one aspect of her behaviour was inappropriate. Not long after I felt the weight of Janet Ainsley's look an incident took place, the ramifications of which disturbed me deeply.

A disciplinary incident arose which was the talk of the store. A woman with twenty years service had, on audit, been found with a till error of £100. She had managed to conceal it by over-counting the gift vouchers and attaching a personal receipt. I knew that this was a temptation which some staff succumbed to especially when they needed money for a short term reason. It was the case with this member of staff. In her defence at the disciplinary hearing she had pleaded that it was to provide a gift for her niece's wedding. The company did have a Benevolent Fund to which staff contributed but she had chosen not to apply for a temporary loan.

Janet investigated the case and I was given the job of taking notes at the disciplinary hearing. It was a difficult case. The woman in question had some minor conduct issues in the past but this was one that dealt with honesty. She knew that she had made a serious error and pleaded length of service and overall good conduct. Janet's recommendation took this into consideration and she recommended to the manager that the woman be transferred to a nearby store and no further involvement with cash duties.

The Birmingham Store Manager was in his late 50's. He had worked for the company all his life commencing as a warehouse worker and progressing through to Management. He was strictly of the old school. He was a decent and fair person and tough on disciplinary issues. He rejected Janet's recommendation and insisted on dismissal. His view was that it was an act of dishonesty and he rejected mitigation on previous performance. He believed that toughness in these issues was the best deterrent. There was nothing wrong with his decision: it complied with company rules. He could have taken a more lenient line – accepting Janet's argument of length of service and previous good conduct - but he did not choose to do so.

The woman appealed but the Regional Manager did not overturn the decision. She was dismissed. From that point, although, she was very careful not to face the manager head on, Janet set about to undermine him. It was subtle.

At meetings she quietly questioned decisions. She damned him with faint praise when talking to other managers. She over magnified the manager's weaknesses when the store had a bad month and she underplayed his contribution when the store excelled.

I watched the performance feeling powerless to do anything and wondered if I should mention it to the Regional Manager but I felt it was not my place; I felt that I was too junior. Janet's strategy might have worked if the Store Manager was more flawed or was not respected by the majority of his team. Some Departmental Managers, whose performances were below par, the Store Manager had counseled robustly but although tough he had been fair. He was hard on the problem, soft on the person. So Janet's strategy failed and it was clear her strategy had not gone unnoticed by the Store Manager. He was an old campaigner and well used to political skirmishes.

Several months later Janet returned from a meeting in his office. She was ashen faced but determined looking. She sat grim faced for a minute or two and then left for half an hour or so. We knew something was up but sensed it wasn't wise to ask. We discovered later that she had visited a few of the Departmental Managers close to her to see who would back her if she complained of victimization. She found that no-one would support her.

We learned that the Store Manager had addressed her actions squarely. He understood that her actions stemmed from the earlier dismissal case but her refusal to accept his decision was a confrontation to his authority. He was clear with her that her act of near insubordination towards her Manager meant that from his point of view she would advance no further under his leadership. She could either request a transfer or remain but he was clear that further disruptive actions on her part would be severely punished.

She transferred within a month.

I reflected on that event so long ago. There was a clear lesson to be learned and a clear principle to follow. I thought for a while and wrote it down:

Principle 1.
The lawful instructions of your Leader must be followed.

When the Leader has come to a decision and discussed it with the team, the team has a right to make an objection but the team does not have the right to overrule it. Any individual who finds that he or she is not comfortable with the decision because it conflicts with a fundamental principle of their own should transfer or resign. It is not correct to stay and seek to undermine the decision or the position of their leader.

Exercise – Principle 1: The lawful instructions of your leader must be followed.

Reflect on the Janet Ainsley story. Have you been involved in any action that undermines the position of your leader? What actions will you take in future to ensure your leader has your support?

Are you aware of any members of your team who may be undermining you? What actions will you take?

CHAPTER 3

Alan Daniels

I read the details of the Janet Ainsley incident, made some minor changes and moved on. I searched my mind for another and within a minute or two found it.

Alan Daniels would be the subject of this story. His story had turned into legend but it was not the kind of story that the company liked to have in its annals. True, the company had its share of historical and indeed current "heroes". These people were publicized and revered by the company for innovation, cost reduction or boosting sales revenue.

Indeed Alan had been one such hero. Alan and I met at many company meetings and conferences. He had left the company five years previously and the story of his leaving was remembered to this day.

Alan was a genial, mild mannered man who had joined the company in his thirties and at age 41 was appointed to the Store Manager position in Edinburgh. His enthusiasm and passion for the business coupled with sensible innovation and a keen eye for what would sell boosted store performance dramatically in the first three years of his tenure.

I was asked to visit the store by his boss to assess what techniques Alan was using which could later be disseminated as best practice to other stores. And the visit was impressive. The report produced had been full of praise for Alan and his team and many of the ideas were recommended for use in other stores.

During the visit Alan had been asked many questions but two questions I regarded as more important than most. The first was: how do you do it?

Alan had smiled at this. "It's not difficult, he replied. "It's mainly that most people after they've reached their target ease up. They start to breather easier. They get satisfied. We don't. We set ourselves a target that is even tougher and then maintain a constant supply of best sellers and find imaginative ways of increasing sales of slow-movers. We're fanatical about costs too, not only staff hours but "shrinkage". We take care of the stock and have zero tolerance for pilfering by staff. All teams are held accountable for losses in their area."

It was clear too, that morale in the store was extremely high. They had the opportunity to be creative and to take a share in bonuses earned. So they were happy on many levels.

Alan was also asked why he did it and he laughed uproariously. When he finished he replied easily to me. "I have a wife and two children and a large mortgage. If my salary isn't supplemented by good bonuses we get by but not as well as I would like. I do it because I need to. I need the money."

I did not put this revelation in the report when I got back. It doesn't sound quite so good when you say someone does it just for the money. I wasn't sure too that I believed him totally at the time. Everyone tends to say they do things for the money and up to a point it's true but I also believed that there is an intrinsic motivation of being proud of doing a job well. I genuinely believed that Alan felt that as well but surmised that he may feel it to be a shade pompous or affected to say so.

We were all totally surprised at the events that unfolded. In the fourth year of his tenure at Edinburgh, Alan simply lost interest. The figures took a tumble in all areas and people from his store started to leave in much greater numbers than before.

Of course, the alarm bells started ringing at the Head Office when figures fell consistently well below target and I was sent up to have a look at things with the Regional Manager. The store looked scruffy and the high morale I'd seen before had disappeared. It was clear that staff needed direction and leadership and a clear reminder of the standards that were necessary day in and day out. Alan had abandoned his responsibility as it seemed to me.

It was clear to me that the Regional Manager was nonplussed. He was also embarrassed and by way of excuse argued that he had thought Alan's drop in performance was temporary. He rarely needed to monitor Alan's store because it was always so good. The look on his face showed that he wished he had visited earlier.

I left the Regional Manager to examine the store and to commence putting things right. I knew where I would find Alan. He was in his office drinking coffee and reading the newspaper. He was very smartly dressed and looked relaxed.

He looked up from the newspaper and said with a smile, "I wondered when you guys would eventually get here. It took you longer than I thought."

"What's happened, Alan?" I asked him. "The store is a mess."

He put the paper down and shrugged his shoulders. "Yes, you were really impressed when you came before, I remember."

"Yes, I was. But what's happened, what's changed?" I repeated.

"You asked me why I did it when you came last time. I told you it was because of money." He smiled effusively and leaned back in the chair. "Now I don't need the money."

Alan explained that he had inherited a substantial sum on the death of his father and he no longer needed to work as intensely, if at all. I could not understand why he simply had not resigned. Why had he allowed the business to suffer so much and desert the people that he led? He was completely indifferent to this and showed no regret or remorse.

"Off the record, I never liked "doffing my cap" to you people," He explained. "I did it because I had to. My father was never going to make an advance to me before he died. I knew that. So I had no choice but to do something that would pay reasonably – and you paid well."

"So you feel no sense of obligation to us and to the people in your team. Forget about us for a moment but don't you owe a debt of gratitude to your team of people here." I asked him.

"I don't feel any obligation to anyone," he replied, again with a shrug. "My view is that you would drop me like a stone if my results slipped if I happened to get ill or for some other reason. I was only respected as long as I performed. The staff here have used me just the same as I've used you – for their own ends. They've done well out of it and they have nothing to be sorry about. The ones that can will prosper without me and maybe will have learned something that they will use in the future."

"I don't think your perspective is true about our company, Alan," I responded and I quoted several cases where the company assisted people with health and other problems. I paused, "I don't think your staff would agree with your assessment either. I think you've let yourself down and those around you who worked hard to help you. Your indifference and careless attitude will have caused them a lot of suffering and we'll have to deal with that. Personally, I think you've acted very badly and for no reason."

He shrugged his shoulders again showing his indifference, "It's a tough life," he quipped and then asked. "So when are you going to fire me. I've been waiting to go for a while and I have no intention of submitting a resignation."

I nodded. I didn't think there was anything further to be gained in more conversation with Alan. I went to a private office and called the Operations Director to give him my analysis. After consulting with the HR Director, he asked me to discuss matters with the Regional Manager and to arrange for him to suspend Alan to allow time for an investigation. This was done and Alan never returned.

His story shook the Board for a while and forced them to reconsider if the Mission Statement, Values and principles did make a connection with all employees. They wondered perhaps if it was just a slick piece of literature rarely read and perhaps haphazardly observed. The collective will of the Board was that the principles and values would lead to an "emotional" commitment to the company through (to use that well worn phrase) "winning their hearts and minds" but in Alan's case this had not happened at all.

Alan's case bothered me over the years. He had no underlying principles or value to connect with. He was willing to appear to hold beliefs, values and principles only as long as it suited him. He would abandon them all selfishly if an opportunity arose.

I thought about Alan for some time and then wrote:

Principle 2: All managers must observe a code of practice that sets out principles and values and which must always be observed.

The manager must have a known set of principles and values and abide by them. They cannot be set aside once adopted.

Once a manager has become a manager he or she must commit to the principles in writing and accept the consequences of peers and seniors if they are abandoned.

Principle 2: All managers must observe a code of practice that sets out principles and values and which must always be observed.

Exercise: Do you know what your principles are? Take a look at the list below and identify up to ten that you identify most closely with.

Below is a list of commonly held values. Add any that you may feel are missing. Circle no more than ten that you feel are the most important to you.

Achievement	*Freedom*	*Responsibility*
Caring	*Fun*	*Risk*
Caution	*Growth*	*Security*
Challenge	*Honesty and Integrity*	*Service to Others*
Communication	*Human Relationships*	*Speed*
Competition	*Individualism*	*Task Focus*
Cooperation	*Innovation*	*Teamwork*
Creativity	*Involvement*	*Uniqueness*
Curiosity	*Learning*	*Winning*
Customer Focus	*Determination*	*Diversity*
Fairness	*Family Time*	*Flexibility*
Respect		

Do you feel any sense of conflict with the values of your company or organization? How does this make you feel?

What do you plan to do about it?

While thinking of a new story my mobile rang.

"How are you now," Diane asked. "Feeling better?"

"Actually, I'm feeling a lot better. I've started writing a book," I replied looking up to cast my eyes over the sea.

"A book! This is a revolution. You barely seem to read a book at all these days and now you're writing one." There was laughter in her voice.

"I know, I know," I replied diffidently, "But I guess it's therapeutic in some way. It is making me feel a lot better and I think I'm grasping at something. I'm not exactly sure what it is yet but if I keep going I'm sure it's going to emerge."

"Ok, well you can tell me more when I get to you, I'm leaving now David – and I've taken the afternoon off."

I did not reply for a moment. I knew that this would have been difficult for my wife to arrange. "Thanks, Diane," I eventually replied. "That's really good. Thanks."

"See you at the Swan," she responded cheerily.

I pocketed my mobile and put away my writing papers. Mentally, I was mulling over a new story leading to a new principle and Clive Stevens, Finance Manager at the Head Office, was going through my mind. I spent a few minutes fixing the events of the story into a sequence, closed and locked the chalet and headed for the Swan.

After lunch – low on red wine – as I wanted to work on the stories again Diane and I drove in our separate cars to the chalet. Diane made it clear that she was not going to interrupt my creative mood and busied herself with domestic tasks in the chalet while I returned to the verandah to write.

CHAPTER 4

Clive Stevens

Clive was and still is a contemporary of mine. We joined the company at around the same time and often find ourselves at the same meetings and on the same training programs and seminars. There are always people at work who you respect for their ability but can't necessarily warm to as far as their personality is concerned. For me Clive was one such. He would be very close to the last person I would want to be on my own with at a restaurant or in a pub.

He was most of the time unsmiling unless he had scored an intellectual victory over a colleague or better still over a senior manager. And this would happen a lot. Clive was very rarely bested on the presentation of financials and very quickly people learned that a challenge to the accuracy of any data would lead only to a rapid climb down. I had to admit that, in all of the time I had known him, his work was frighteningly accurate.

I wish I could say the same was true of mine! However, because of his coldness and arrogant display of his intellectual superiority he was most often avoided by his peers unless it was strictly necessary to engage with him. In fairness to him he did not court the favour of senior managers or use his knowledge to belittle his peers publicly or privately. Rather he quickly pointed out the error in thinking, in a school masterly fashion, checked that his point had been understood and moved on.

He loved his job and although promotion came his way, it could be seen that Clive accepted it as a logical conclusion to his effort. Like some, he had never "wandered the corridors" seeking to network with those who could smooth his advancement. He would get it on ability or not at all. He had a "take me as I am" mentality. He indulged in no office politics, did not network and had no friends at the office.

He always took his lunch at the staff restaurant and normally ate alone. He had a passion for Greek and Roman literature and while eating would read oblivious to all else. Occasionally, he would be interrupted by one of his team needing urgent advice or an explanation. He would never show any sign of irritation at being interrupted but would deal with the issue, explain clearly and satisfied that the individual had understood would return to his book. Whatever amusement or laughter which rose up in the restaurant, his absorption in his reading never ever led to his raising his head out of curiosity to see what was happening. Or maybe he did hear but was not sufficiently interested to take a look.

Nobody knew much about his family life. He did not bring it to the office. We became aware that he became married purely because of an application for marriage leave and over the years the arrival of two children was again only noticed through leave applications. There were no family photographs on display in his office and he never mentioned his family life or vacation to anyone.

On one of our occasional weekend late nights in London, Diane and I saw him and his wife at a restaurant where we chose to dine. He waved over at us politely but made no attempt to socialize. Later when a band at the restaurant started up, I noticed curiously his dancing was a picture of wild abandon. It was the total opposite of his work personality.

His staff neither liked nor disliked him. I guessed he would be indifferent to their emotional reaction to him in any event. He had no favourites and treated them fairly. He rewarded achievers and corrected poor performers and those he perceived as not trying. He did this dispassionately and the office gossip marked him as "firm but fair". Noticeably all but the very tough – whether his staff or not, whether a manager or not – felt a twinge of apprehension if making a visit to his office. Did people really adjust their ties nervously and swallow just before going in? Yes, some of them did.

He was regarded as a safe pair of hands, if a little cold. However, I believe it was his lack of real affiliation with his team that was the problem.

Every manager and leader needs to support their team and protect them from others who may be using their power or position unfairly. Once Clive became a manager with a large team, some people spotted a chink in his armour. It might have been nigh on impossible to upset Clive's equilibrium but some realized that he would do nothing to defend his team.

I first realized that something was not right when a casual remark came from one of my team during a review meeting, when she said with a chuckle, "you may not be perfect, boss, but there's a lot worse - rather you than Clive Stevens, for example."

"Pardon," I asked curiously but she muttered that it was just a joke, a little embarrassed to continue further. "I didn't press the issue but I was taken aback. If she had mentioned one or two other managers, I would not have been surprised."

I thought no more of it until I noticed a group of five or six of Clive's team at a table in the staff restaurant in a huddle discussing something in hushed whispers. They fell silent when Clive walked in and selected his food items and went to his usual table. As usual he gave barely a cursory nod to anyone including his own team.

I was alone myself on this occasion and reading a journal. Nevertheless I could not stop myself from observing Clive and his team. Something was clearly taking place. The team were now just looking at one of their number, Jeff Erickson, a Finance MBA man in his late 20's brim full of confidence. He was well respected, I knew, and seen to be a rising star in the Finance Department. However, on this occasion, he looked a shade nervous as he got to his feet and walked over to sit with Clive.

Clive looked up with no emotion showing on his face and waited as Jeff Erickson took a seat along side him. It was apparent that Jeff was making a request to discuss something with Clive. At first Clive's features seemed as impassive as ever but then I noticed a rare and fleeting look of surprise.

I could see that Clive had no intention of discussing the subject in the staff restaurant and he put his hand up to halt Jeff's flow of speech. Clive looked at his watch and I guessed that he was agreeing a time to meet with Jeff later. Jeff got slowly to his feet and returned to his workmates. After a while they all dispersed returning to their workplaces. They had thought it best to tackle the lion out of the den, I thought. But it seemed he was no easier outside of the den, in a benign location.

I continued to read my journal but occasionally glanced over at Clive. There was no doubt in my mind that he was not his usual tranquil, untroubled self. He was reading but every now and then his concentration seemed to break and he became lost in thought for a minute or two.

After a while he gave up the attempt to read and got to his feet, placed his tray on the trolley rack and started to leave. He caught sight of me and I smiled and nodded. For a moment it looked as if he was going to walk in my direction but he changed his mind, waved in acknowledgement and left.

Much later that afternoon I decided a visit to Clive's office might be worthwhile. It was around 6.30pm and many had left. There were a few of Clive's staff milling around but not in the usual numbers. His Department usually worked late.

I found Clive unusually leaning back in his chair, hands behind his head, staring out into space. I greeted him and in doing so broke his reverie. He nodded showing no surprise at seeing me. I can't say I was a frequent visitor to Clive's office in keeping with many others.

"How are things?" I asked cheerily. I took a seat at the front of his desk.

Clive did not reply for a while and ignored my greeting. "Can I ask you something?" he looked at me seriously.

I was going to say, "What me? Give you some information? This has to be a first" but I didn't. I wasn't sure if Clive would see the joke or appreciate it.

"Go ahead," I responded and waited. He took his time thinking over what he wanted to say. When it came, the question was a long way down.

"I believe I'm very good at my job," he began. "I've worked with the company for a long time and served the Departments well and also saved the company a great deal of money and made a great deal of money through various initiatives. I'm proud of my work."

He paused and I nodded, grunting my agreement and signaling him to carry on.

"I've always stood on my own two feet, never asked for help from anyone and dealt with any conflicts or challenges to my judgment on my own. That's right, isn't it? I've never asked for you help, David, have I? Or anyone else's for that matter."

"That's true," I responded.

"Yes, it's what I believe and I believe others should do the same?" he went on looking at me to see if I agreed so far.

"Go on," I encouraged.

"Jeff Erickson came to see me today. I respect this young man. He's very bright and will do well."

I nodded in agreement and waited.

"He was speaking on behalf of my team, he said, Clive continued. He got to his feet and started to pace the room. "He said that everyone respected me for my knowledge etc, etc, but they couldn't deal with the fact that

I did not use my position to support them and protect them from other senior managers' demands."

He stopped and waited for me to say something. The picture began to open up for me. I could see in my mind and maybe I'd also seen it in reality that people went to his Department to harangue junior staff for information or to complain. I could see that Clive would never intervene.

"They have to fight their own battles, don't they? If they have applied themselves and know their job and work thoroughly they will succeed. That's how I did it. No manager came to help me fend off others. I had to deal with it myself."

"But we are not all like you," I thought.

"He said that he's considering resignation and so are a few of the others," he continued but his words now seemed more directed to convincing himself. "They have good jobs, good conditions, are paid well and I see that they get good bonuses."

"What if they are not as strong or as gifted as you, Clive?" I asked him. "What if they don't have your mental toughness also?"

This stopped him in his pacing. Was it a revelation for him or was he mulling it over?

"Whether we like it or not, Clive it's all about relationships and the obligations within those relationships. Maybe with your team you might need to think about your obligations as their leader". I said it slowly and quietly.

Then the big question finally came. "What do you think I should do?" he asked.

"Clive," I replied with a smile. "You've never had any problem working out the solution. I think you can with this one too."

Clive gave a rare smile and held out his hand for me to shake. I shook the hand warmly. Maybe he's learning about relationships after all, I thought.

During the next weeks in my visits to the Finance Department I witnessed a transformation in morale. Clive had taken the right action and kept an eye on transactions taking place between his team and visiting managers from departments. Clive's measured walk when he sensed conflict between one of his team and someone from another department often resulted in a speedy resolution without him having to say a word.

In a way he reminded me of my brother in that ability to see off a potential conflict.

Principle 3: Defend individuals in junior positions who are unfairly or harshly treated by those with power.

A leader has a duty to defend his or her team and anyone junior who may be suffering from harsh and unnecessary treatment from those who have greater power.

Principle 3: Defend individuals in junior positions who are unfairly or harshly treated by those with power.

Do you feel you do enough to protect those around you who are junior? Do you feel yourself unprotected by your leader?

What actions will you now take?

CHAPTER 5

Kathryn Ellis

"I'm going to work on this every evening for a few weeks if you don't mind darling," I called out to Diane. "And also out here on the weekends. I need to finish it."

I knew there would be a silence before the reply.

"That's fine with me, but we're not going to leave you alone. We'll spend time with you out here on the weekends without disturbing you."

"That's great", I responded. "I need to get some time in with you and the kids also."

I found myself wondering if we find it difficult to trust these days. Despite all the evidence that someone is a trustworthy individual an action of theirs out of the ordinary is often looked upon suspiciously.

If we see a colleague with someone of the opposite sex taking lunch together eyebrows are often raised. If someone takes a day off unexpectedly or unusually calls in sick we can get suspicious. They must be attending an interview elsewhere!! If someone doesn't answer their mobile or respond to an sms within seconds we can get suspicious.

It's curious isn't it, I thought, that if we get called to the boss's office for an unscheduled meeting the initial thought is, "Have I done something wrong?" It's rarely, "Am I about to be rewarded?"

With these thoughts in my mind I picked up my pen to write about Kathryn Ellis.

And so Kathryn Ellis raised suspicion. Kathryn was and in fact still is the Area Manager for the London District. She was a lifetime, dedicated employee for our business. What Meredith Belbin would refer to as a "Company Worker". She was never seen in the category as one of the company fast track rising stars who could produce results way above expectation. (Interesting though that these rising stars or "incendiary devices" often move on once they've racked up enough achievements on their CV to attract another company).

In Kathryn's case she genuinely loved her job and the company. She was loyal, hardworking and with unswerving honesty and integrity: a woman of deeply held principle. She consistently delivered a solid "B" performance and although she was not an innovator herself she quickly assimilated new ideas and adopted them with success in her area.

Kathryn was reserved and a woman of few words. This did not mean that she was shy or antisocial but rather she did not like to speak excessively. She preferred to speak only when she felt that what she would say would add value and make a contribution.

A few years ago we both attended an in-company "Business Strategy" training course and we sat next to each other for the few days duration of the program. As with most courses there are one or two delegates who want to speak at every opportunity hoping to impress the most senior "important" delegate present. Sometimes too they hope to impress the program leader convinced that their "outstanding contribution" will be brought to the attention of career shapers.

Kathryn, however, was a listener and a not a talker. She focused keenly on the concepts and ideas raised by the tutor and when she asked questions they were pertinent. When she commented her remarks were relevant and incisive.

I felt that some people thought she was too withdrawn and maybe overly serious in her personality. People found it difficult to "label" her. They knew she was not married and never had been. She was in her mid 30's and as far as anyone knew she had no partner and very little was known about her personal life. At social functions she would attend and circulate sufficiently but leave when she felt that the obligation had been discharged. She never drank too much at these occasions and her behaviour was always impeccable.

With her own team she was "firm but fair". Most of her team were at first curious about her management style and gave up trying to get close to her. What was absolutely certain was that they respected her immensely.

On one occasion, I overheard two of her managers discussing her style. Their collective opinion was that Kathryn, unlike many people, did not set out to win the popularity of the team. She was indifferent to being liked.

She focused on good results and great customer service, reviewed people's performance impartially, coached where necessary to improve performance, praised good performance and weeded out those who were not prepared to contribute. However, before the weeding out process was activated she did her best to motivate, re-educate and correct the performance of the individual. She was delighted if the individual responded and saddened if they didn't but had no hesitation in resorting to termination if there was no attempt to improve. Kathryn had no favourites.

You cannot say that she was a charismatic leader because she was not. She was a quiet leader who set the example for performance and expected others to match it. It would be impossible for her to follow the "hail fellow well met" style of leadership intended to jolly people along to achieve results. I sensed that she found this style too disingenuous, too artificial for her taste.

I think Kathryn saw things in different terms. She had a contract of employment – as did those who worked for her – and she fully intended to deliver on the obligations of that contract. In turn, she expected those around her to do the same.

She possessed in abundance the quality of gravitas.

This did not mean that her face was unemotional, granite like and cold. She would beam with pleasure at the achievement of her team, radiated empathy when discussing the work or home difficulties of a team member and her laughter was unabashed when listening to a joke or an amusing incident.

So why would anyone be suspicious of this caring and responsible manager? Surely, if there were anyone to trust it would be Kathryn.

And yet suspicion did fall on her.

Quite by accident the Operations Director and I met up in the office reception area very early one Monday morning a few years ago. He surprised me by asking if I would join him in his office for a coffee as soon as I was ready. Ten minutes later I sat in his office sipping from a streaming mug of strong, black, Colombian coffee. He came straight to the point.

"I'd like your opinion on Kathryn Ellis and her work," he requested and gave me a steady, piercing look while he awaited my reply. I repeated everything that I've written above and he nodded his agreement with each comment I made.

"Yes," he responded becoming lost in thought. "You've summed up exactly what I would have said myself."

"But you are changing your opinion…..?" I prompted.

He shrugged his shoulders as if in doubt. "Well, it's nothing really and maybe I'm reading too much into it." His face in fact did show some guilt as he spoke, aware that he doubted one of his stalwarts.

"So, tell me," I urged him on, "What's happened for you to have these doubts?"

Now, at that time, our culture was one of complete dedication to the company. Long hours and availability at all times were admired as much as great performance. The Operations Director had tried to contact Kathryn by telephone in the early evening two or three times in succession. It wasn't that late about 6.30pm and she hadn't answered and did not return the call until very late. When he had called her for a meeting on Friday at 6pm she had said that she could not attend but would come in on Saturday. He complained that this arose on the following Friday also.

"Well, it's hardly major stuff," I said to him, a little surprised at his obvious suspicion. "Did you ask why she wasn't available?"

"She said it was for personal reasons," And it was clear from his body language and facial expression that he was more than a little miffed that she was not more explicit about the reasons.

"I think you're reading too much into it," I counselled him. "It really is nothing earth shattering or anything to be concerned about."

"Yes, I know you are probably right. With anyone else I probably wouldn't bat an eyelid," he argued and obviously uneasy with his viewpoint. "It's just that a few months ago if I asked Kathryn to come in every evening for a meeting between 7 and 10 she would have agreed without hesitation."

He looked at me a little anxiously and then broke eye contact looking down at his desk.

"So you want me to find out if anything's wrong, I assume?" I asked smiling at his downcast expression.

"Would you?" he responded quickly and with almost disbelief. "I can't ask anyone in my team and I know you are very discreet."

'I'll get back to you," I said and left.

I found some reason to be at Kathryn's office the following Friday at around 4pm. It wasn't too difficult. Her Regional Office was based at our flagship store on Oxford Street. I spent some time looking at the merchandising and layout of the store and discussing sales figures and buying trends with the manager. Once this was concluded I asked the manager if Kathryn was in her office. On finding out that she was, I took the staff elevator to the top floor where the regional office was based.

We don't like to have closed and concealed offices in our company – unless it's for Directors – and I could see Kathryn working at her PC through the glass windows of her office. I knew several of her regional staff, and we exchanged greetings politely as I walked to her office.

I felt a little guilty about this 'quest' and wondered why I had agreed to it. I stood outside Kathryn's half-glassed door observing her working and the strength of her concentration. Why would anyone think that Kathryn could be lacking in trust I thought. She leads, manages and sets an example in the very best way.

I couldn't stay outside the door observing her indefinitely and so I tapped the door to gain her attention. A slight frown crossed her brow at the interruption and she raised her eyes to see me at the door. There was a fleeting look of surprise at my presence but then she smiled warmly signaling for me to come into her office.

As I entered, she rose from her seat, came out from behind her desk and she shook my hand like an old friend. She gestured for me to take a seat in front of her desk and occupied the one next to it.

We exchanged pleasantries and chatted idly for some minutes until Kathryn with a wry smile asked me, "You've come to check up on me, haven't you David? Someone has sent you."

Are there occasions where being untruthful or devious can be allowable? In most cases, I think, the reason is often because we wish to escape some embarrassment, pain or argument and concealing the truth temporarily may achieve this aim. Nevertheless, I did not wish to be disingenuous.

Kathryn's look was so sincere, natural and straightforward – penetrating as well – that anything other than the truth would have been a minor debacle. She would have seen through me quite easily.

"It's not checking up, Kathryn, "I stumbled for words. I wished that I had planned and thought through this discussion before arriving. I felt somewhat inept and clumsy.

"Don't they trust me after all these years, David?" she said with a playful, not antagonistic smile. "One change in my routine and I become a suspect."

She laughed brightly. The situation amused her.

"I'm sorry, Kathryn. It's really not like that." The thing is perhaps it was. I'm not sure the overall concern was for health or welfare but rather she was not as reliable as was the case before.

"David, it's my personal business and nothing for the company to be concerned about," she commenced and watched me closely. She went on, "You don't know a great deal about me, do you?"

"Not just me," I answered honestly, "I don't think anyone in the company does. You don't seem to have a close friend or confidante."

"They wouldn't be that close or a confidante if everything I said was passed on. Would they?" she challenged humorously.

I smiled, admitting defeat.

"David, I'll make it easy but then I'd prefer not to discuss it further and for it to be left alone. Is that understood?" Kathryn's tone was serious and insistent.

I nodded my agreement.

She paused, breathed deeply and looked inwardly for a moment before beginning. "My family is and never has been that well off. Our family is traditionally from the working element of the population. We work in factories and shops, building sites and parks. My family is one that works with it hands. Education was for other people, not for us. By some quirk of nature school, education and understanding came easily to me. In my family I was something of an oddity. They didn't know whether to be proud or embarrassed about me."

She paused to renew inwardly some old memory or incident and then went on." My father died in an accident on a building site when I was 10 years old. My mother did a wonderful job bringing up my sister and I. She worked at Boots as a Store Assistant for years – and all the hours she could get – to make sure my sister and I were fed and clothed. She died six years ago of lung cancer. She'd always smoked and nobody could convince her to stop. My sister and I have always been very close. She was three years older than me and like my mother she went to work at Boots. She married very young when she left school – one of her school boyfriends – and they were happy. They would have loved to have children but it wasn't to be. Last year she died of breast cancer. She'd had a mastectomy 8 years ago and been clear until last year. Then it returned but in her bone. They tried to slow down its progress but the end was inevitable."

She stopped to reach for the glass of water on her desk and took a few sips. She looked at me, concerned for a moment. "I forgot to invite you to take tea or coffee. Would you like?" She reached for the phone.

"I'm fine" I responded and waited for her to continue.

"At the funeral, I met up with one of my school friends. She'd remained in touch with my sister all through her life, but I didn't know. She said that she thought I was in a different class now and that we would have nothing common. You know, I literally pictured two classrooms with no inter-connecting doors. In a way maybe it is like that. She is a single mother with a 9 year-old daughter who is so bright. I decided to help with her education and I've set aside some money for her to go to a private school. I visit their home each Friday evening to spend time with my friend and her daughter. I can't go any other time because of her job and mine. It's Friday evening or nothing. So my Friday evening is now sacrosanct."

Kathryn stopped again and smiled. "That's it, David. Nothing earth shattering just a realization that there is more to life than work and my decision to give something back: to help someone. It could be a charity but for me this is more personal, more direct and the results are visible."

"But why didn't you say what you were doing when it first arose?" I asked her.

"I wanted to keep it private if I could. This was something that I didn't want any gossip about. I've achieved that so far in my career here, haven't I?" She looked at me, folded her arms and cocked her head to one side.

"Yes, you have," I spoke softly to her. "Kathryn, you really put us all to shame. You really do. I'll deal with it now."

It was one of those rare occasions where I ignored office protocols and embraced Kathryn warmly before I left. It felt the right thing to do but I did wonder what the office staff would make of it. Awful, isn't it that innocent actions that celebrate the humanity of us all may be manipulated malevolently by others?

I left feeling uplifted by Kathryn but with a vague sense of dissatisfaction about myself and my conduct. I decided that maybe I needed to look at my own behaviours and decide if they were still in line with my brother's advice all that time ago. Had I slipped in any way, I wondered.

I called the Operations Director and arranged to meet him the following Saturday morning. We met and I retold the story but received his guarantee that it would not be talked about. He, like me, felt the same disquiet about our conduct in this case. It was our conduct that was at fault and we knew it.

The story has a good ending. Kathryn's actions changed our focus. The Operations Director discussed with the HR Director the idea of encouraging our company and managers to provide selfless acts of charity in their local communities.

It touched a chord with our employees. It was and it still is a huge success.

Principle 4: Provide personal and financial help to a family, group or local charitable cause for which you have an affinity. It should be with personal involvement and not remote financial help and should not be publicized. It is a selfless act.

All managers should find a charitable activity outside the workplace to help others. It does not necessarily need to be financial aid. It can be selfless assistance that will help others with no expectation of anything to be received in return.

Principle 4: Provide personal and financial help to a family, group or local charitable cause for which you have an affinity. It should be with personal involvement and not remote financial help and should not be publicized. It is a selfless act.

Exercise: Do you live your life inside a bubble regardless of the needs of others around you in society? It is easy to donate cash remotely to help others but what can you do by volunteering and become personally involved.

What actions will you now take?

The Kathryn Ellis story finished and I sat back. The recollection of the events had stirred up memories that affected me. Was it possible that I may have slipped in my own beliefs and intentions if not for the sharp reminder from Kathryn of the importance of principle in each area of our life in work and out of it?

"Hey, David" Diane called shaking him from his reverie. "I'm interrupting you because you've stopped now. I've been watching you for a while. You can really bang the keys at speed."

I laughed. "I've got a lot to say. Any way, what time is it?"

"Time we left!!" Diane chuckled and waved her car keys in front of my eyes. "I asked the kids to raid the fridge for their meal and to order take out if they wanted."

"Let's go home then," I responded and gathered all the things I needed. "It's Saturday tomorrow so I'm going to get up early and come here to start work again."

"You are bitten by the bug, David, my husband", Diane said with a laugh. She held me by the shoulders. "Or are you working off some guilt through therapeutic writing?"

The children chided me in good humour when we returned home. When I explained what I was doing they were further amused that I was actually writing. Like all clever children they negotiated a promise from their father that I would deliver when I finished my writing. Of course it involved me spending cash on them.

The following morning I rose early, showered, took breakfast and left the house quietly without disturbing the family. I drove to the chalet and while driving, I considered the next principle and I looked back over my working life to seek the person I needed and their act. I nodded to myself. It was Brian Chapman.

CHAPTER 6

Brian Chapman

Brian Chapman was a young graduate recruit like myself. He had been working for the company for just about a year when I arrived. He made a point of coming to see me on my first day and invited me for a drink with him after work.

"I'll show you the ropes," he said with a smile. "What they like here and don't like, what you can get away with and what you can't; who are the real influencers, movers and shakers – and who's going up and who's going down."

In those early days, Brian was a tall athletic young man who played rugby on the weekends. He was hugely sociable, with a massive smile and uproarious laugh. He had a swathe of blonde hair that he continually flicked back from his eyes.

He was waiting for me at the office entrance when the day was over and took me to a local pub about ten minutes walk from the office. Brian was an easy talker and a swift drinker. He was hugely interested in my early life, school and University career, where I was strong in character and abilities and where I had weaknesses. He was particularly interested in what my fears were in joining the company. I mentioned to him that I was terrified of giving presentations and desperately hoped I did not make a fool of myself.

Over several pints he chatted seemingly inconsequentially about these things and true to his word he gave me some information about the way the company worked and the senior people in the company. He was scathing of most of the managers and Directors with a couple of exceptions.

As the time passed that evening I had a feeling that Brian was an ambitious, cocksure young man who was determined to get ahead. He certainly had the confidence and the presence. We parted on good terms and I thought about much he had said on my journey home.

The following morning Denise Ashton, the HR Manager, who had been assigned to organize my induction into the company commented on my socializing with Brian.

"I saw you leaving the office with Brian Chapman last night," she remarked with an amused grin on her face. I nodded. "I'm sure it involved a few rounds of beer."

"Of course it did, Denise" I responded laughing. "Neither of us is married or has serious relationships and that's what young guys do after work. Go for a beer."

"Be careful, David. I'm sure he got to know you much better last night than you did him," she commented knowingly and more seriously. I shrugged my shoulders and thought no more of it.

During the day Brian passed by my floor and called to see me. He arranged for us to have a few drinks with some of the other younger people from the office after work. I was glad that he was helping me to integrate so quickly into this new work environment.

Once again he met me at the office entrance and this time we walked to a local pub a few minutes closer to the office. There were five other young graduate entrants (three men and two women) already in the pub. We joined them and Brian immediately took command.

For me it was a salutary lesson. Throughout the evening Brian regurgitated the information I'd given him on the previous evening and presented in such a way that it mocked many of the things that had happened in my life and was mildly derogatory of my skills and weaknesses.

At the time I found it painful. I felt let down by this seemingly charming young man who, I thought, had wanted to help. The opposite was true. He simply wanted to dent my confidence and to make me appear dim-witted and mediocre in front of his entourage.

"Don't worry about it" one of them turned to say to me while Brian went to the bar. "This is Brian's attempt at an initiation ceremony. He'll only pick on you now periodically. He moves around everyone in turn."

When I'd had enough of the clever sarcasm I decided it was time to leave. Brian, of course, took on an attitude of mock-offended and as I left I heard his uproarious, jeering laugh as I left the pub.

I reflected on the incident over the days that followed. It was clear to me that Brian was an intelligent bully. His ferocious ambition led him to seek to neutralize any opposition by intimidation. He sought out the weaknesses of others and exploited it ruthlessly. He gave offence to achieve a superiority and domination. His offensiveness and sarcasm were veiled by humour. His intent was clear. The implication was that he was not to be taken seriously. He was only joking.

I decided that his company was not necessarily for me and despite his attempts to get closer and to get me to join his circle in the early weeks, I resisted. As he realized this, the smile on his face did not diminish but the smile in his eyes did.

His chance for retribution came during my first six weeks in the company. I was due – along with others - to give a presentation as part of my induction program. There were four of us scheduled for the presentation that day. Brian, being the character he was, had let everybody know that I feared presenting and that he would do his best to help me overcome my fear before the event. He also let everybody know that he would be there to support me. Well, I did say he was clever.

He did, of course, offer to help but his eyes said everything. Denise Ashton had drilled us well on presentation skills and so I practised, practised, practised. I'd also come across, quite by accident, books by Norman Vincent Peale. I liked his concept of "imaging", that is imagining yourself doing a task very well and focusing on that outcome alone.

So the outcome was that I put in quite a good performance. This was despite Brian's attempts at off-putting while I was preparing – whispering behind his hand to the person next to him and winking at me. Throughout the presentation he leaned back in his chair with folded arms and eyeballed me. A smirk of disdain was ever present on his face during the 15 minutes or so of the presentation.

At the end of the presentation he asked two difficult questions but I dealt with them effectively. In the comments to all of us at the end he said, "David Adams seemed the least prepared and the least confident but it was passable."

As I left the room when the event was finally over, I heard Denise say to Brian, just loud enough for me to overhear, "If you prepared as thoroughly as David maybe your performances would be as good." I didn't look back. I could guess the look on his face.

Over the few years that followed there were many instances of Brian's offensiveness.

If somebody had a lisp, Brian would imitate it when speaking to them.

If somebody were of less than average height, Brian would make a comment.

If somebody were "thin on top," Brian would smirk.

If someone were not as confident as himself, Brian would find a way to intimidate.

If somebody's clothing were a shade off style, Brian would make sure they knew.

If someone made an error at work or fail to reach a key target, Brian would come to sympathise.

If someone suffered from a skin complaint, Brian would screw up his face in mock sympathy.

How did he get away with it? Why wasn't he tackled about his offensiveness? Because he was very cunning. It always operated on the edge of humour or as mock empathy. Also, he was exceptionally good at his job – creative, innovative and he could spot an opportunity. He made money for the company and so perhaps his offensiveness and inappropriateness was overlooked. Also, he was careful only to focus his sarcasm on those who did not have the power to harm him career-wise.

His business success did get him a promotion four years after being with the company and again his performance proved to be good. He knew what he was doing. There was no doubt about that.

Two events, however, took him beyond his normally careful execution of his sarcasm.

Philip Anderson, his Head of Department – his boss – suffered a tragic experience. His wife was killed in car accident leaving himself and two teenage children. Not surprisingly, this affected his performance and he probably went off the rails for a little while. It was common knowledge that grief hit him hard and one Friday evening after work in the company of a senior colleague he drank way too much. He was not boisterous or rowdy and he caused no trouble but he consumed drink after drink until tears of grief trickled unbidden and unnoticed by him continuously from the corners of his eyes.

Later, his friend and fellow senior manager, argued that he needed this and that he had decided to stay with him until he had let his grief come out. In any event someone from the office witnessed the scene and watched him walk unsteadily from the pub supported by his friend.

He was away from the office for three weeks after this and when he returned it was clear that although scarred by the experience of his loss he had recovered most of his inner strength. He had the full support and sympathy of the Board of Directors who had always respected Brian's contribution to the business. It was perceived as – and was exactly how I felt – a case of "there but for the grace of God, go I".

Brian it seemed watched carefully, as exploiting weakness in competitors was his specialty. It was unusual for him to seek to make an attack on a senior manager but perhaps he felt that His Head of Department had already received a savage wound and might be easy prey.

A few weeks after his return, Brian decided to make a strike. It happened during a Friday afternoon meeting when Philip was reviewing the activities of the week. The account of the meeting was told to me later by one of the attendees. It so happened that Brian had completed a key milestone in the department objectives ahead of time and under budget. Philip was pleased and singled out Brian especially for praise at the achievement.

There were several good things that had happened that week and the mood of the meeting was good humoured and relaxed. As the close was reached, Brian said, "Well, we've done so well we should celebrate now."

There were the usual sounds of positive agreement from some and murmurings of "at another time" from others. "Come on, Brian urged his eyes twinkling, "The boss knows how to party so let's go for it until we want to dance and cry with laughter."

It was a cheap shot and the good-humoured mood of the meeting fell away rapidly. Philip had a fixed smile on his face and looked steadily at Brian. "Yes, I'll lead the way, Brian, and as you've made the invitation we'll all be happy for you to pay."

They were carefully chosen words. Philip had drawn a line.

Shortly after this incident Brian's second error arose. His attention had wandered to a newly recruited young woman in the Accounts Department. She was married and in her mid 20's. She was prone to attacks of acne for some reason that covered her cheeks and forehead for a while and then healed. At the time of the incident she was awaiting to take treatment with a new drug designed to eradicate the problem.

One evening, Brian came across her with some of the other Accounts staff at the pub close to the office. He left his own group and joined the Accounts group. After his initial pleasant behaviour and humour, he started to sympathise greatly with her skin condition and talked about his own acne sufferings as a teenager. Brian's complexion was such that it was clear that hardly a blemish had made its way onto his face. In his usual way, he progressed from sympathy to subtle rudeness and the young woman was badly embarrassed by him. He left when he felt he had done enough damage to her confidence.

Encouraged by her friends she decided to make a complaint to HR about the incident and it triggered an investigation into his behaviour.

This had never arisen before as Brian had always managed to avoid such investigation and he was confident that nothing would happen. His bravado and braggadocio continued and in front of his friends he showed no signs of slackening up. A week later, with his friends in tow, he observed a group of girls at the pub who attracted his attention. Maybe, he had decided to show his resolve to his friends that he was undeterred by the investigation and so he commenced a conversation with one of them. As usual he sought first to gain attention and then to be rude. As his behaviour started, a well-built man in his late 20's stepped away from the bar and interrupted Brian.

"I think you should apologise to the girls for your behaviour," he suggested to Brian.

It was not the first time that Brian had met such an encounter and he knew how to play it. He swiftly apologized if he had caused any offence. He made it clear that sometimes he went too far but there was no harmful intention on his part. He was deeply sorry if he had caused any pain. To a casual observer his apology would have seemed deeply sincere.

However, the large man was not to be put off. "You think you're very smart, don't you?" He looked at Brian with disdain. "You seem to get your kicks from embarrassing and humiliating people every chance you get."

Brian started to protest but the large man would not be put off. "People like you need a lesson sometimes."

Although, Brian was reasonably well-built and fit himself, he was no match for this man. The man hit him twice and Brian went down. The girls that he was taunting burst out laughing and his own friends smirked openly. It seems everyone felt he had it coming.

The large man stood over him, with hands on hips, waiting to see if Brian wished to continue. From his sitting position glancing at his friends and the girls, he saw that no help would be forthcoming from anyone. He scrambled to his feet and left hurriedly.

The large man apologized for the incident to those in the vicinity and especially to the girls that Brian had been taunting. He said that he could not abide such cruelty as this man had shown. They applauded him as he left the pub.

It was later discovered that this man was the husband of the Accounts clerk with the facial skin condition. He had decided that he needed to confront the man who insulted his wife and dented her confidence.

Of course both incidents were the talk of the office at that time. Curiously, most people felt that physical violence was no way to deal with a problem in the civilized world and yet they could not help feeling delighted that Brian Chapman had taken a beating from the husband of a woman he had insulted. How could a seemingly wrong act be regarded as right and applauded by many?

Brian lost what support he had and resigned within a couple of weeks of the incident. I never discovered what happened to him and never saw his name feature again with any of our rival companies.

Principle 5. No manager should ever give offence to any person within or outside the organization. Personal attacks based on different personality, race, religion, physical appearance etc. are not to be tolerated.

We are all required to work across multicultural and diverse groups. Association with others is based on respect and mutual trust and we should never knowingly harm or hurt others through word or deed.

Principle 5. No manager should ever give offence to any person within or outside the organization. Personal attacks based on different personality, race, religion, physical appearance etc. are not to be tolerated.

Exercise: Do you use your power in any way to humble others or do others do so to you?

Brian's case is an extreme example of course but what actions do you plan if you feel it applicable?

I often thought about the incidents surrounding Brian. Particularly, I wondered why, although it was regarded as wrong for the husband to have punched him, that there was a sense of rough justice in the act. I wondered if the incident had ultimately made Brian re-think his attitude. Wherever he was, was he now living his life as an individual who did not give offence? Would he have done so without being brought to his senses in this way and the exposure to extreme embarrassment? It was a conundrum with which I have often found myself wrestling.

I took a break to make a cup of coffee and thought about my next principle. I knew it would cover the areas of optimism (positive thinking) and courage. These were areas that also had a profound effect on people in teams. As I sipped my coffee, my thoughts turned to Claire Ellis.

CHAPTER 7

Claire Ellis

Claire Ellis was recruited as a graduate entrant from Cambridge where she'd achieved a first in English Literature. I remembered having a discussion with her during her training. She learned extremely quickly and in a short space of time acquired detailed knowledge of how the company worked and what made it work. She quickly gained a reputation for her encyclopaedic knowledge and her peers would seek out for clarification of some detail or procedure that they might not understand.

She had decided to seek a position in the HR Department and was accepted. In the early years, her knowledge of procedures and her research were helpful to her managers. Yet in those early days, she was not necessarily responsible for making things happen.

I did notice after a while that Claire was something of a loner. She did not seem to have close friends amongst her graduate peer group and had not formed any real friendships at work. I noted this but did not regard it as a particularly worrying as everyone has their own working style. Some people did only seem to form light almost acquaintance style relationships at work and formed deeper relationships outside of work.

I realized some time later, however, that Claire's isolation from others was not necessarily self-imposed. It seemed that others were not overly keen to share her company. For, as people came to know her, behind her detailed knowledge they discovered a person who rarely laughed, was unsmiling and who would predict the worst possible outcome for any situation. She seemed to focus on bringing bad news to people and focused on problems rather than solutions. Not many people like their day disturbed by pessimistic thoughts and so they tended to avoid her company unless they were required to interact with her on a work level.

Because of her knowledge she was given the job (similar to a promotion) of HR Team Leader for Store Opening. She had a team of three to assist her in all HR activity connected with the store opening and was a member of the main Store Opening Team. This was always Operations led and the Operational members produced the detailed time line of activities required for completion. Clare's activities were provided to her in broad details but it was her and her team's job to interact with other teams to provide a more detailed sub-plan and timelines that integrated with the overall timeline.

During my career I had been involved as part of the Store Opening Team at various levels. They were always enjoyable, fast moving, demanding quick decisions and opening to the agreed time. We'd done it many times and had the procedure covered in all areas. The main lesson you learned from the experience was that the feasibility study would be a "snap shot in time" and that circumstances change. As time progressed after the feasibility study new information became available which could change or vary the product mix or staffing levels and in other departmental areas too. Nevertheless, any changes were all within the predetermined area for the store.

To paraphrase a military expression we were required to: analyse, adapt, improvise. If you slavishly followed the plan more often than not you'd be making an error and we all knew that.

Claire's first involvement in store opening was for a large out of town facility on the edge of Cardiff. The first task she set herself was to understand the feasibility study thoroughly. And she did.

For the first few meetings all went well. The store was under construction and members of the team were working on their detailed plans. As meetings progressed and operational team members started to make adjustments to product mix and areas assigned to departments, Claire started to get anxious.

"But the plan doesn't say that," she would remark. "It will cause us a problem. It will delay us."

The Operational Manager, in overall charge of store opening, understood her inexperience and sensed her anxiety. She, as other members of the team did, reassured her that it was a normal part of the adaptive process.

However Claire was trapped into following a route pre-determined by the study. It was strange she could see that errors required fixing in the study but she did not share the creative energy of others to find a solution to the problems encountered.

Because of her inability to adapt to the changing circumstances and her continuing negativity, the overall Store Opening Team Leader lost patience with her. Her usual style of involving others in the problem and allowing them to generate a solution ceased to apply with Claire. She was instructed what to do and told to follow it to the letter. She also met with the HR Director to discuss Claire's inability to adapt and her negativity. She also informed the HR Director that she was convinced her attitude was affecting those members of her HR Team who were assisting her.

The HR Director didn't want to over react and said as much to the Team Leader. The HR Director argued that Claire was still on a learning curve and perhaps they had included her in the team more quickly than they should have done. Nevertheless her breadth of knowledge had been a factor in her selection for the job. The HR Director suggested that her progress be kept under review as to replace her at this stage might seriously undermine her confidence.

The HR Director did have a meeting with Claire and became aware of Claire's focus on problems rather than solutions. She did see the flaws in the plan but seemed unwilling to depart from it. I thought about this much later and realized the basis of her thinking. She did indeed recognize the plan needed changing but if it was followed and did not work how could she be blamed. In fact she could claim it as a success because she had predicted that this would be so. However, if she adapted it and it did not work then she would share the blame. She could not seem to have belief in herself and the positive outcome. The pessimistic outcome was easy to follow and indeed easy to achieve. The optimistic and positive outlook demanded more flexibility and adaptability and was a greater risk.

Much later in my discussion with the HR Director we agreed that keeping her on the project at that point was probably a mistake. However, we could not at that time realize how firmly rooted she was in her pessimism, negativity and failure focus.

Everybody on the team persisted with Claire but in reality they marginalized her. Her own team were the most demoralized because they wanted to co-operate and make suggestions for improvement but without Claire's consent they could not. The result was that the Store Opening Tea merely gave Claire and her team instructions without seeking their involvement. Neither was Claire involved in the wider discussions of the project.

When the instructions were given to Claire she accepted them with a pained look on her face. Her attitude was "if that's what you want us to do we'll do it, but we are not convinced it will work. I'll do it but when it fails it's your fault not mine."

As a store comes closer to completion in stages members of the Opening Team temporarily move location to the city or town and work from a nearby hotel to implement the final stages of the plan. This was the case with Cardiff and Claire and her team were required to do so to implement the phases of the manpower plan, induction and training program. Although team members were required to interact with Claire on a work basis, they avoided her in the evenings. She was effectively excluded from any social activity. If she tried to join a group to sow seeds of doubt she was rebuffed. Her team members were accepted by the others and became involved in social functions. Claire found this hard to deal with and her relations with her team deteriorated. In the last stages of the plan they asked her to be re-assigned.

It was at this point that the HR Director asked me to look at the situation and advise. There was no alternative but to return Claire to the Head Office and appoint one of her team as the HR Team Leader. Claire's reaction was typical of one who constantly expects the worst outcome. "I was waiting for this," she said to me without emotion. "I had a feeling that something like this would happen."

Without Claire's negative attitude and failure-based focus, the Store Opening Team breathed a collective sigh of relief and got on with the job completing on time and with some superb innovations that modified the plan.

In my reflections on the incident I was drawn to the writings of Norman Vincent Peale. He makes the point that for a positive outcome, knowledge is alone is not enough. It must be coupled with persistence and a strong belief in being able to achieve the desired outcome. Claire most certainly had the knowledge but lacked the last two attributes with a potentially devastating effect on her team.

Claire did eventually recognize that her negative and failure focus attitude was not helping her and she sought help from HR to attend programs designed to address this problem.

Principle 6: A positive attitude, determination and self belief are essential in ensuring that a manager can work with a team to fulfill objectives.

We cannot enter into any activity without positivity, energy and enthusiasm that we use to inspire our teams. If we cannot do this, we should choose not to lead people.

Principle 6: A positive attitude, determination and self belief are essential in ensuring that a manager can work with a team to fulfill objectives.

Exercise: Do you arrive at work at all times with a positive attitude and a determination to work with others collaboratively to achieve goals?

Is there anyone on your team who needs guidance in this area?

What actions do you intend taking?

It was now lunchtime and I paused for a while. Claire's case was the example I remembered most largely because "she had slipped through the net" of the process which selected individuals to lead teams. Nevertheless, I had met many other cynics and failure focused individuals who were able to disguise their belief more successfully than Claire. They were the ones who voiced behind the senior manager's back "that this will never work" and to the manager's face the same message but thinly veiled as "I'll give it a go then" or "I'll try my best." For some, the pessimistic route was easy, David thought, because it required no effort. The outcome was self-fulfilling.

I took a walk outside and along the beach to think about my next story and the next principle. The walk helped me to think about my next subject – David Wall. David had come to the company with a reputation as spotting a good bargain and driving a hard bargain. As he worked in purchasing these were much valued skills. David could not help smiling when he thought of him. David was a charming man, a bon viveur, a chancer with an immensely attractive bearing and personality. He had charisma.

I started to write.

CHAPTER 8

David Wall

David Wall simply loved money and everybody knew this. I could not remember a time when it was not on his mind. It seemed that all his actions were in some way leading to a financial benefit for the company. This was his forte.

David had previously worked as Head of Buying from one of our competitors. He was well known in the business and the life and soul of the party at retail conferences and exhibitions.

His admirers said that he attracted people to his table or seating area who then buzzed around him like bees at a honey pot. Those less endeared to him, who may have been motivated by jealousy, combined words such as rats and drainpipe. David Wall: there were those who loved him and those who wished he were anywhere but in their range of vision.

So for sure David was an imposing man of about six foot tall with classical handsome features, thick black hair with hints of grey appearing. We recruited David in his early forties. His smile was warm and broke out easily whenever he met a friend or contact and doubled in intensity when he met somebody who was a potentially new addition to his list of contacts. He wore dark designers suits with crisp white or blue shirts, startlingly coloured but fashionable ties and highly polished black shoes which never ever showed a hint of wear at the heel.

David was the consummate negotiator and persuader. He read body language with ease and his eyes were always working tactfully to discover information from a room in an office, a corridor, meeting room and the words said or left unsaid by those he met. He was also gifted at reading upside down!

His notes following a first meeting with a potential supplier were packed with information. He had the ability not only to gain information with his eyes but to disarm the person with whom he was engaged in conversation so that he was provided with remarkably good intelligence. His predictions of outcome following such a meeting were astonishingly accurate.

David was, of course, bemused by the astonishment of his team and peers. "It's not that difficult," he would exclaim with surprise, "Use your eyes and ears and ask the right questions at the right time and you get information. Simple, right?"

He was of course proud of this ability and especially that it was not matched by anyone he knew or anyone in our business. This gave him an almost supreme, unrivalled position. Indeed, there is no doubt that his work made a very real difference to the bottom line of our company.

But David was not one of those characters who kept his techniques and skills to himself. No, not at all. He enjoyed coaching the members of his team and sharing his knowledge and skills with them. He made a habit of accompanying individual team members on visits and observing their performance first hand. He closely questioned the individual after these business visits and discovered what they had learned and taught them to see what they had missed. It was not critical: it was helpful. He taught each person how to improve and do better. When his techniques "clicked" with them and their success soared, he was as delighted as they were.

He genuinely seemed to care about their development and progress and willed them to do well. It was unusual. Many managers then and now only go so far in sharing the secrets of their achievements. David went the whole way.

And because David made it an edict to himself to communicate well with his peers and seniors, he made it mandatory for his team also. His message to his team was to pay as much attention to the "customer service" required from other internal departments as they did with suppliers. His philosophy was that relationships with other departments were equally as important as those with the supplier. He reminded his team that poor relations with other Departments could often affect the quality of the work provided to his department and perhaps lead to costly delays. "Make them your friends", he would urge, "just as much as you seek to make the supplier your friend. Some of them may be jealous of your earnings and so an occasional small gift or lunch for those who have helped you will work wonders."

I smiled. In his quest to ensure he had the co-operation of all peers and seniors he had on a couple of occasions invited me to lunch "to pick my brains". Ah! Yes, David was a skilled business diplomat, polished and adept with his dealings with all and he managed the act without appearing the slightest bit disingenuous.

When questioned on his unusual willingness to develop his team so well David smiled. He argued that their collective success led to greater company profitability and in doing so enhanced bonuses for them – and as he was their leader for him as well.

David was the most consummately skilled networker and achiever that I have ever met in my working career. His antenna never stopped working to source new information and new possibilities. And all the information he gained he shared with his team, his peers and his superiors.

Nevertheless, it was obvious that he quietly reveled in their astonishment at the information and success he achieved. His department buzzed and many looked on in envy at the team spirit he created. He was seen as a management exemplar: he just simply did everything right. It would not be untrue to say that he was a master craftsman in his profession.

Thus it was that David's achievement and his team's achievement resulted in not only exceptional annual bonuses but also in the triggering of regular quarterly incentive payments. David was extremely well paid and his lifestyle reflected the size of his income. He wore designer label suits, shirts, ties and shoes and drove an expensive car and although his position in the company entitled him to Business Class travel he routinely upgraded to First Class. In most cases he did this by sheer persuasion but where it failed he willingly paid the difference from his own pocket.

He loved the style and the image he displayed. Of course he justified the upgrade to First as an opportunity to network with top-flight decision makers and there was some truth in this. But also there was no denying he loved the First Class treatment and all that it entailed.

He lived in a fashionable and expensive part of London. His wife was an associate professor of economics at one of the prominent London Universities and their two young children both attended one of London's most expensive private schools.

David was totally devoted to his wife and children and he consistently remarked that his sole motivation for working so hard and so effectively was to give them opportunities and a lifestyle that he had not been given.

To sum David up: he was diligent, motivated and a hard working achiever, a good team leader who treated his staff fairly and retained the right amount of distance even taking account of his "bon viveur" lifestyle. Despite his charisma there was never one whiff of an inappropriate relationship even though he may have had the opportunity. All in all, he was a talent to be admired.

Perhaps it would always have been so. However, at one year end David did not receive the bonus he had calculated based on his Department's achievement. Additionally his responsibilities were increased without an addition to his base pay.

In fairness to him he probably did deserve a little more bonus that year than was awarded but his revered negotiating and persuasive skills did not achieve the amendment he sought either in bonus or for increased responsibilities. David might have left his boss's room with a regretful smile and with the apparent determination to right this perceived wrong against him through another year of enhanced performance, but developments proved this not to be the case.

David's focus on money led him to take a large private commission from a supplier who had been trying to work with him for some time. The person he dealt with was subsequently fired from his company for some indiscretion and he turned to David for help. David was either unable or unwilling to do this and as a result the person took revenge by sending to our company a videotape of the negotiation between him and David as well as a clear visual of David accepting the money.

David was suspended while in an investigation took place and then dismissed. There is no doubt that his involvement in this act astonished those in the company who knew him. There was nothing in his prior behaviour that could have predicted it. Nevertheless, in reviewing all his actions it was clear that everything he had carried out was purely for and only for financial reward – even in his development of others.

Principle 7: Value achievement and the development of others more than personal reward.

Every manager needs to earn financial reward to exist but it cannot be the only reason. All managers must develop others and focus on achieving results for the organization that they serve.

Principle 7: Value achievement and the development of others more than personal reward.

Exercise: Ask yourself the question if money comes first in your organizational life and blinds you to real achievement and the development of others.

What do you plan to do to improve in this area?

I stood up from the laptop after completing the David Wall story. I smiled realizing that I was getting into the rhythm of writing. Glancing at the time I calculated that even with time for a coffee break I could manage another two chapters that afternoon. While making the coffee I started to think about Jennifer Webb. It was an interesting theme. I returned to my desk with the coffee.

CHAPTER 9

Jennifer Webb

Jennifer Webb is a Manager in our HQ HR Department. She is intelligent and knowledgeable and very ambitious. I got to know her very well because when she joined us she was assigned to me for three weeks as part of her induction program.

At that time, Jennifer was 27 years old and following graduation from University she had joined a well-known UK supermarket chain as a graduate entrant. She gravitated towards HR as her specialism and, indeed, her knowledge in this area was formidable. I quickly realised that we had gained quite an asset from the supermarket chain.

Jennifer was an only child and the pride and joy of her primary school teacher parents. They encouraged her to take a business rather than academic life and after she had graduated from London University they were delighted when she made it onto the graduate scheme in the supermarket business. While there she also enrolled for an Executive MBA and studied part-time.

During the years that followed, she exuded calm efficiency, knowledge, great people skills and an unerring knack of applying her knowledge appropriately for each situation that arose. Moreover, she thirsted for stories of best practice and kept well up to date by reading specialist HR and Business magazines. She had a talent too for translating HR practices in unrelated industries into section of our business with great success.

This "creative swiping" often earned her commendations as well as good financial reward.

Yet despite her great people skills within the HR Department Jennifer was a "lone wolf". She would be in the team but not of the team searching for all the information she could gain for her personal advantage but rarely sharing her findings with others. There are perhaps many people like this who are afraid to share what they know because of some view that in doing so they will give an advantage to the other person.

Most of us learn that through co-operation and sharing and building good relationships it helps us to achieve more and also helps others to achieve more. On the surface, Jennifer appeared to subscribe to that view but in return for work-related help and co-operation from her peers she was likely to provide friendship, social and personal help. She was careful not to provide help and information that would enhance the performance and effectiveness of a peer, close colleague or subordinate.

Now why would that be so?

Plainly and simply I realized, eventually, that not only was Jennifer incredibly ambitious (and in being so saw many people as competitors) but also she was driven solely by money. It seemed as if it was a race to her to get above everybody else to establish that she deserved a higher position, higher incentives and higher reward. This wasn't apparent straight away. It did take a while for these characteristics to emerge. The fact is that the majority of people in an organization are not driven to be super-achievers in the same way that the majority of people in organizations do not want to do a bad job. Most people want to do well – as well as they can – but to be a super-achiever demands exceptional focus and more. To step from being a good strong achiever to an exceptional achiever at a relatively young age demands that the person increases knowledge, gains skills quickly and sharpens the ability to make connections between knowledge, skill and the circumstances and culture which pertain in the organization. This is not easy to do.

The longer a person stays with an organization and moves through the various employment stages from apprentice to master craftsman it becomes easier to move from good achiever to high achiever. The ability of the individual to make links becomes more rapid and some may become more intuitive. It takes time for this process to work through but if, as in Jennifer's case, the person is focused and driven to get through the stages quickly, then it is achievable at a younger age.

Does it come at a cost? Well I think it depends on the circumstances. In Jennifer's case she shared nothing. In the end no matter how much the individual seeks to conceal it, failing to follow an honourable principle ultimately affects the individual adversely. It may be hidden for some time, but as the individual progresses in the organization and becomes more visible the betrayed principle becomes more evident. It starts to glow like a blush on the face of the person.

And so it did with Jennifer.

She was on good terms with a lot of Store Managers and often formed focus groups to explore and search for new ideas. At one of these focus groups, a relatively new Store Manager – Anne Ferrer - came up with an idea. She did not have the confidence to share it with the full focus team at that time and spoke to Jennifer privately about it.

Most HR Departments get concerned about sick absence levels and measure it furiously seeking to find what can be done to help and assist if it is genuine. However, some are not really sick and as one commentator put it some years back just "sick of the job". It's true that at this time our sick absence policy was tough and indeed so was our policy on leave days off. Anne Ferrer argued that, knowing the toughness of our leave policy, many people took time off disguised as sick leave to attend to urgent personal business – caring for a sick child, accompanying a close family member to hospital for an appointment etc. She argued that many people would take a day's leave or even leave with no pay to be allowed to deal with this personal business. However, the system didn't allow it. Therefore, some staff found their own way. They went "sick" but they didn't just take a day off, they took a few and kept it just under the serious state of formal warnings. To take one day might lead to a connection with a family emergency, so employees took more. Ann Ferrer argued that if we were flexible with time off for emergencies we would see a measurable drop in sick absence and improved morale.

To be fair, Jennifer could always recognize when she was on a potential winner and so it was with this case. In conjunction with Anne she developed a new policy and procedure for dealing with these matters and gained approval to run a trial of the system at Anne Ferrer's store. It was a success. Anne's belief proved to be true and there was measurable decrease in absence. True, paid and non-paid leave days increased but overall costs decreased substantially. There was a knock on effect too in that employees actually felt that Anne's policy did recognize the emergencies in their life and overall commitment to the business improved substantially. It showed itself in many areas and especially in improved customer service. If your Manager has just knocked you back it's hard to deliver service with a smile!!

Based on the trial, Jennifer obtained approval to roll the concept out Region by Region and in each area the same improvements were observed. The revised concept saved us a lot of money and made us a lot of money. Jennifer was well rewarded. However, she did not attribute any credit to Anne Ferrer. When the company newsletter eventually featured the scheme and its success and gave an accolade to Jennifer it had consequences.

Every single employee at Anne's store signed a letter to the Chairman that assigned the credit to the scheme not to Jennifer but to Anne. The letter made its way to the HR Director who started to investigate. Jennifer would not back down. She was willing to admit that she had discussed the idea with Anne to further the trial at her store but not more than that. It has been my belief before and since that when this arises, the individual involved really does believe this. The true origin of the idea is forgotten.

Of course the whole episode affected Jennifer's reputation and the relationships with those around her. The incident arose a couple of years ago and Jennifer is still with us but it's probable that she will seek another position outside soon. Colleagues, peers and other associates are a shade more guarded with her than they were in previous years.

Principle 8: Ensure credit and reward is fairly shared with all the team.

It is the duty of leaders to develop others and encourage ideas. The ideas should not be stolen and a good leader ensures credit is given to and publicly acknowledges the originator of the idea.

Principle 8: Ensure credit and reward is fairly shared with all the team.

Exercise: Review your performance in this area. Do you really ensure your team gets the credit for all achievement?

Does anyone on the team selfishly take credit for the work of others?

What do you plan to do?

Finishing the Jennifer Webb story I sat back to think about her. She was a very good person at heart, but the desire for selfish recognition at the expense of others had distorted the situation and she was now not trusted fully. It was a shame.

And that led me on to thoughts of Kevin Parsons. And what a character he was!

CHAPTER 10

Kevin Parsons

Thoughts of Kevin Parsons always made me smile. He was an extremely personable man who dealt well with all customers and his staff. He had a knack of defusing a situation and the ability to get to the heart of a problem and find a solution.

Kevin Parsons was a fast track young graduate who reached the position of Area Manager very quickly. He was around 28 years of age at the time of his appointment and destined for higher positions.

He was from a working class background. None of his family, prior to him, had made a great success at school but Kevin broke the tradition. He did well at school, obtained good GCSE results and went on to get excellent A level grades. He wanted to attend University but knew that this would be difficult and he would get limited support from his family. He had struggled to convince his family that he should go on and do A levels. To go further to University was passively resisted by his parents but he did it anyway.

He once told me, “I don’t really think their reluctance was to do with us needing money. It was a fear that I would be gone forever. That studying for a degree would take me through a door that would never lead me back. I only realized this in hindsight. Working back here is great for my family. I work in a “shop” like my mother did. They are comfortable with that.”

He told me that it was hard in his community to appear as if you were a "swot" or a "boffin". You were a hero if you cocked a snook at authority figures and showed you didn't really care about school-work. "The point is," he went on, "I loved it and I saw it as a route to a world I only saw on TV or in magazines. Peer pressure is harsh when you live in a tough community. I had to balance between showing the right degree of mischievousness and working enough to get through my school-work moderately well but without doing too well. I managed it in the end."

Kevin went on to acquire a first class honours degree in Business Studies and Marketing from one of the strong red-brick universities. He was originally from the North East and proud of his Geordie accent which he had modified for it to become accessible but giving a clear statement that it would never disappear.

Over the years, I had met Kevin on a number of occasions at training sessions and also where he had given presentations. His character was strong and he was persistent and determined. He was not given to elaborate speaking or frilly presentations. He was a plain speaker using logic and emphasis to make his point. Kevin liked simplicity and doing the basic things extremely well. This was his Cri du Coeur when dealing with his Store Managers.

It worked well and Kevin consistently ensured his stores gave a solid performance. None fell into the category of those requiring special attention. Kevin displayed a gritty confidence in dealing with his Store Managers many of whom were older than him. However, he did not display cockiness or arrogance nor patronize his Team. In fact the reverse was the case. He was quite clear in his dealings with them that he did not know all the answers and he was clear that he had a lot to learn from them. His low-key style with his team worked well. He did not distance himself from a Manager who had erred and more often than not took the blame for an error that could have been attributable to a Store Manager. Equally, if an idea emerged from his team that was successful he made sure the Manager received credit for it. They loved him for this.

His management style was to allow freedom of expression and decision making within the core principles of the company. He encouraged people to use their instincts, think what worked locally and what was original. He never dictated that things should be organised in a particular way to an experienced Store Manager. As long as the results were on or above target he believed that he had no reason to do so. He focused on those who needed his help.

And that was the way he liked to be managed too. I think we all do unless we are inexperienced and need guidance.

However, there came a time when Kevin faced a serious challenge to his thinking. The Operations Director appointed a senior Area Manager on a temporary basis to trial a new system to assess store performance and productivity. It was trialled in three of our areas, one of which was Kevin's.

Throughout the development Kevin disagreed with aspects of the system and made known his views within the group and more widely. The senior Area Manager was patient and experienced in dealing with opposing views. She tried several tactics to win Kevin over but he could not be convinced and would not implement in his area.

She passed by my office to discuss Kevin's refusal to comply. She was reluctant to visit the Operations Director to tell him of the outright refusal although there was no doubt in her mind that he knew of Kevin's opposition.

"If I take it to the Director," she said," It becomes official and I have a feeling that Kevin will just dig his heels in and not back down. The consequences will be very serious for him."

"I'll visit him tomorrow and let you know what happens. Maybe we can get him to see reason," I told her.

I didn't call him beforehand of course. Just arrived at his office. He didn't give me a broad smile but rather a self satisfied grin as if he was happy that he'd stirred something up.

"You've been sent to persuade me to participate," Kevin laughed and sat back in his chair fingers tapping on the desk. He was enjoying it.

"No, I haven't come to persuade you exactly, Kevin. Rather, I've come to seek your resignation." It was said without a smile and stopped Kevin from tapping his fingers.

"Are you serious?" Kevin asked exploring my face for signs that it was a joke.

"Kevin let me tell you a story that I learned long ago from John Garnett who at that time was Director of the Industrial Society." I sat down at one of the chairs in front of his desk." He was leading a course I attended then. He solved a problem simply for me – and one that you are facing now. He told us that when our boss sought opinions and a course of action that we should openly speak up and voice views assertively. It is the boss's job to evaluate what is said and then make the decision. Sometimes the boss will ignore all that is said and make a decision that takes little account of the views given. That is his or her right. And Kevin, this is the important point – he told us at that point we faced a choice. Once the boss had made that decision and informed us we had to leave the room and carry out the instruction as if it were our own! If we could not do that, he told us, that the only honourable thing to do was to resign. No other option was possible if you were not on board with the decision."

I stopped speaking and waited for Kevin to think about what I'd said. He thought and then spluttered, "But it's not a resignation matter. The trial can take place in the other areas."

I raised an eyebrow. "Kevin you've been given an instruction so now you have the choice."

He sat back in his chair and pondered for a while.

"Kevin, the object of a trial is to evaluate and make a judgement on what works and what doesn't. You're putting yourself out on a limb for nothing.

Just like me if you're given an instruction you have two choices. Now are you on board ....?" I left the other words hanging.

"Ok, I'll do my best."

"Kevin, I don't like those words. 'I'll do my best and I'll try always means you are forewarning that it's not going to work. Remember, you have to carry out the instruction and deliver as if it were your own."

"Ok, David. I've got the message. I'll do it. I'll do it!"

In fairness to Kevin, he did. It always seems easy to us doesn't it: to choose the instructions we want to carry out and ignore those we don't. When it comes to the final conclusion we have democratic input in defining a decision and helping to shape policy but the boss always has the final say.

Principle 9: Support and follow the instructions of your boss

As leaders we can and should make our point of view known and argue our case strongly. This is what makes for better decisions but once that decision is made the arguments are over and we move to implementation. No one has the right to undermine and sabotage a senior's lawful instruction

Principle 9: Support and follow the instructions of your leader

Exercise: Review your interactions with your leader to determine if you follow instructions with enthusiasm.

Do your team follow your instructions with enthusiasm?

Consider the current situation and the actions you will take.

I was really pleased with the work of the day and indeed I wondered why I had not "put pen to paper" before. I found it an enriching and enjoyable experience. I closed the laptop and packed away to drive home. I found myself really looking forward to an evening of entertainment with Diane and my children but also I was looking forward to returning to the chalet to continue the exploration of my theme – Finding Nobility.

After Diane and the children left for work and school respectively I savoured the extra minutes in bed. It was a luxury and somehow felt like a "guilty pleasure". Normally, I would have been up and out of bed two hours earlier in time for the commute to work. This extra time really did feel luxurious and comforting.

I rushed through shower and breakfast, feeling a sense of urgency to get to the chalet and commence my writing. Thoughts were already going through my mind and accelerated during the drive to the chalet.

I was thinking that these days it has become more or less fashionable to be independent, self-sufficient and see peers as competitors. Less opportunity for promotion because of flatter structures and knowledge that you won't be in the job forever has led maybe to looser and more competitive relationships with peers. But the truth is that we need to support all in the team. It is probably true that when we join a team we position ourselves accordingly in a hierarchy of capability and identify the weakest link. Once we have done so, it is probable that the thought that goes through the mind is "If anything goes wrong or gets complicated then he or she and not me will get the blame". This of course is a bad strategy.

Thinking of this has put in my mind the case of Sally Walsh. I had the plan of my writing clearly in my mind as I arrived at the chalet. While parking my car, I could see just a few people as usual strolling the beach and at that time in the morning there was still a little chill in the air.

But my thought were on writing and after unlocking the door to the chalet and opening my computer on the desk I started to write.

CHAPTER 11

Sally Walsh

Sally Walsh was a fiercely competitive HR executive in the HR team in London when I first met her. She joined the company through the graduate programme. In her case she gave me much cause for reflection on how the education system may not prepare individuals for the challenges at work. Although there is some collaboration between students on various projects and they attend lectures and tutorials together it does not simulate the real requirements of people interaction at work. Indeed, ultimately the individual student is on his or her own as it depends on the effort they put in themselves to pass examinations which determines success. For that, there is no collaboration or working with others to achieve a goal. It is all individual and from an early age it seems that pupils and students are measured against each other and often streamed in order of perceived capability and examination scores.

It is hardly surprising then that many people arrive at work with the impression that achievement arises from individual effort alone. Whereas personal effort at work is a prerequisite, it almost always interlinks with the work of others. So many arrive at work needing to learn how to collaborate and not compete with others as they strive to achieve a common goal.

We probably added to this in the early days by having a performance management system that was force ranked and linked to bonus. This perpetuated the mistaken belief that peers were in competition with each other. Everybody wants to be A rated and to get the highest bonus and maybe this encouraged some to keep an eye on those around them and maybe, just maybe, hold back on certain information. It made me wonder if there was a secret smile if a 'competitor' made an error and stumbled like a runner in a road race.

And indeed, Sally was a highly competitive person. She was working in my team in the Headquarters and I hired her because of her intelligence, knowledge and energy. As a matter of course, I included others in the team in the selection process. This is not necessarily a formal process but involvement in a group meeting to discuss a particular problem. It gives an indication of the interpersonal skills of the potential new hire and lets me know how well they are likely to fit in with the team. Needless to say the team members will also give feedback to me on how well they think the candidate would fit in.

In Sally's case her interview and tests were excellent and she was thoroughly gracious when we ran the meeting to discuss a few items. I could see by the smiles of the team that they felt she was someone they liked and who would fit in with us. Maybe, I should have picked up one aspect of that meeting which did penetrate my consciousness at the time but I let it pass assuming that it was just an eagerness to impress and be offered the position. I noticed, that after each contribution, she glanced my way looking for some reaction to what she had been saying.

At that time there were four Managers on my team and twelve in total. Sally was hired based on her performance in the selection tests and interviews but I encouraged her to move on after one year with us.

The work of my team of Managers was interconnected with a great deal of reliance upon one another and collaboration with one another. Once Sally's trial period ended she adopted a different style.

On the surface she appeared friendly to all and certainly made a great effort to obtain the support of her own subordinates and those of her fellow managers. However, the first indication of misgivings was a subtle slight on the work of one of her peers. On handing in a piece of work at a meeting she said:

"I hope you like this work. The contribution I received from Rachel Todd was not bad but I made some additions to it to improve the quality."

The implication was lost on me and, at that stage, I simply responded to her that I was surprised as her colleague's work had always been of the highest standard.

A series of incidents took place in the months that followed which included dropping comments to subordinates regarding the work of her peers and failing to provide the necessary information to her peers to enable them to make correct decisions. She often sought and used one on one meetings with me to highlight the problems with others and to complain that the others were no longer being friendly towards her. There was no doubt that the quality of her work and the speed in which she completed a task was exceptional but it was always at the expense of others.

The team work and spirit which I had built up carefully was being eroded but more than that, the team was beginning to think that I was tolerating her divisive behavior because the quality of her work was appreciated. Sally was only interested in helping one person and furthering the interest of one person and that was Sally.

In coaching her she could not see that her comments regarding the work of others was inappropriate. She could not seem to see that supporting her colleagues and assisting them was an important part of her role in the team. As far as she was concerned her only concern was that her work was perceived to be of high quality and better than the work of others.

It is probably true that whatever team we are in that we are only as strong as the weakest link in that team. It is maybe a human trait that people in teams look for their level. It may also be true that some people look to see who is the weakest person in the team and who may be at risk if something goes wrong in a project or if a restructuring is to take place. Yes, when this arises, the behavior of the team and the leader of that team is dysfunctional. Of course there are levels of ability within any team depending on experience and skill. Yet the duty of that team and the leader is to coach and develop all to a higher performance. For one fact is probably true: all of us one day regardless of our skill and experience will find ourselves in a team in which we are the least capable. And when this arises, our thoughts are always: I hope the others will help me.

In Sally's case, she neither saw any need to collaborate with nor to assist others and after several coaching sessions, she was encouraged to find a new position.

She found a new position easily enough in another company which was no surprise given her capability. Her last act of great teamwork in her last days of employment with us was to complain to the CEO that she had been frozen out by her peers!

We heard that a similar departure took place from the company she joined. I kept a watch on her progress as a behaviour like this derives from character and that is very hard to change. In fact it will only change if someone eventually "sees the light" or can no longer stand the pain of the behaviour.

Principle 10: Support your Peers

There is no competition with peers. Leaders must know that we are all one team and that internal conflicts and lack of support lead to lack of focus on the customer, whether that is external or internal.

Principle 10: Support your Peers

Exercise: Review the current relationship with your peers and your level of collaboration. Do you believe it is of the highest quality?

What actions will you take to improve it?

I also thought that it was sad that Sally behaved the way she did. She was such a talented individual but by no means a team player. I often wondered if we could find the origin for this in the educational system where ultimately all students are taught that achievement is through personal and individual effort. After all, the results posted on the wall list individuals with individual scores from top to bottom. And then these same people join organisations and are exhorted to be team players!!

It made me smile and as I sat back in my chair and glanced over at the beach and the surge of the waves I thought of the selfless Nalini Devi and her encounter with Kate Spelling.

CHAPTER 12

Kate Spelling and Nalini Devi

In part of my career, some years ago, I was placed in a Regional HQ in Manchester. It was one of those locations where a major store was in the same location as the HQ. Very often, the General Managers at stores like this find it to be a nuisance as it is easy for Regional staff to visit unless strictly controlled.

The CEO of the Region, Kate Spelling, was very proud of the performance of the Manchester store and in fact the General Manager was highly innovative and as a result the revenue turnover and profit of the store was the highest in the country. In truth, Jane probably spent more time at Manchester than was really necessary. It was a high performing store and arguably her attention should have been elsewhere assisting other General Managers. However, she seemed to enjoy basking in the success story of this store

There was no doubt that Kate could be a difficult character. She was the highest graded executive in the Company outside of London. She was highly ambitious and proud of the fact that, as a woman, she was competing every effectively in an area where female CEO's were not prominent. She probably had the most sophisticated antennae possible for detecting up and coming female talent and identifying a possible threat to her supremacy.

It seemed that in this context that fate had sent her a challenge and that challenge was in the person of Nalini Devi. Nalini was of Indian extraction but born in the UK and educated at Oxford. She possessed a combination of high intelligence, incisive thinking and extraordinary empathy with all those with whom she came into contact.

At the Regional Headquarters in Manchester, Nalini held the position of Regional HR Director. She occupied the position before Kate Spelling was appointed to the position of CEO. I often wondered if this would have been possible if Kate Spelling had been the Regional CEO at the time of Nalini's appointment.

At that time, I was not a high ranking executive in the business and sent there to learn more about distribution and logistics within the business. Nevertheless, it was a relatively small Regional Headquarters with around seventy people in the various functions. Today we would regard it as an anachronism and as an unnecessary layer of management but nevertheless I found it very useful as a learning experience.

As we were a small unit, I would often find myself at some larger meetings where both the CEO and the Regional HR Director were present. It was obvious that they were not friends although the meetings were always cordial but with a cordiality which lacked warmth. Kate Spelling was a tough, harsh women and prone to impulsiveness when it came to taking action on any perceived disciplinary breach.

The difference in approach between the two women was that Nalini, although being tough, judged each case on its merits taking into account length of service and prior record. She weighed things up and the consensus amongst managers and staff was that she was "firm but fair".

The fact that Nalini was more intelligent and more highly educated than Kate Spelling may have rankled Kate. Kate was reasonably well educated but whereas you could describe Nalini as 'an elegant and skillful fencer' Kate

Spelling was more of a "streetfighter". Thus it was often that verbal battles between them at meetings pitched the dancing of Nalini against the slow, steady advance of Kate who was waiting for the moment to spring and bring her down. But as much as Kate advanced and sprang she always seemed to be clutching nothing but air. Nalini was far too skillful to be caught.

Eventually, there came a moment when Kate Spelling thought she would be able to outwit Nalini. An incident arose which did not become public but knowledge of it circulated throughout the Regional Office.

The Regional Finance Director reported a discrepancy to the CEO and Nalini at the same time. It was clear that Kate Spelling believed she had an opportunity to demonstrate her superiority.

The facts of the case were this: For direct reports to the General Manager at the Manchester Store an allowance existed which could be used for car loan, medical care, school fees, club fees or whatever according to life style. During one of her frequent visits to the Manchester store, and after a particularly good year from the Manchester team, the General manager requested an increase in this allowance. Kate Spelling had the authority to vary such allowances based on regional needs and within a specified limit.

These allowances also applied to senior employees of the same grade within the Regional Headquarters and shortly after Kate Spelling increased it for Manchester one of Nalini's team applied the same increase to Regional Headquarters staff.

It seemed that this was the moment that Kate Spelling had been waiting for. She demanded that Nalini carry out an investigation and to provide her with a recommendation. Nalini did so and involved the Finance Director in the task. Her conclusion was that the action that had taken place was an unfortunate error but that it arose out of logic. She argued that bonuses were personal according to achievement but that allowances were common to same grades in the same geographical area. She argued that it was unfortunate that her department had not been involved in the approved increase to the local Manchester store. If they had been it would have been impossible for an error to arise, as the HR recommendation would have been for the allowance increase to be applied geographically. She stopped short of placing the reason for the error fairly and squarely with Kate Spelling. She concluded that in this case of alleged error there was no case to answer.

It seemed that Kate Spelling did not like the answer and responded that, in her opinion, it was typical of the sloppiness of the Regional HR Department. She demanded that the investigation now been turned into a disciplinary matter and that, if proven, the perpetrator of the mistake should receive disciplinary award and a financial penalty.

Nalini was silent for a few days and subsequently wrote to Kate Spelling arguing against the need for a disciplinary investigation and for the first time stating that the error lay within the CEO's office for amending the allowance without reference to HR. She went on further to explain that the woman involved in her department who increased the allowance for Regional staff was a single mother with a young child and that child was experiencing a very difficult medical condition. The mother was involved in considerable personal expense to assist her child and Nalini stated that she had no intention of adding to the woman's burden as to do so would be grossly unfair.

She went on to say that as Head of the Department she took responsibility for all perceived failures that may have arisen and if the CEO considered a financial penalty needed to be applied then it should be deducted from her own salary.

This seemed to place the CEO in a difficult position. It seemed she could not continue with her pursuit of the disciplinary award for the HR employee yet she seized upon the willingness of Nalini to face a financial penalty personally. She wrote to Nalini tersely but applauded her honour in accepting the financial penalty. She indicated that this would be one month salary and the Finance Director was informed to make the arrangements.

Nalini did not respond to Kate Spelling's decision. As far as she was concerned the punishment of one of her team would have been grossly unfair. She was happy to face the financial penalty.

Much later we heard that the penalty was never applied by the Finance

Director. He believed that this decision was grossly unfair also and simply put the request to one side and never spoke about it and never acted upon it.

It will come as no surprise that Nalini never spoke about it, but within the Regional Headquarters, her status rose and that of Kate Spelling declined. Nalini had acted with honour and fairness and Kate Spelling had not.

No one knew if Headquarters ever got to hear of the incident but a few months later Kate Spelling was transferred to London to head up a section dealing with overseas development.

Principle 11: Resist meanness, unfairness and deceit

No leader should ever take decisions that are intended to embarrass or punish another unfairly. Power over others needs to be exercised lightly and with absolute transparency. To do otherwise is a flagrant abuse of that power.

Principle 11: Resist meanness, unfairness and deceit

Exercise: Review your own behaviours at work and indeed in your life generally. Do people regard you as mean, unfair and deceitful? Do you see these characteristics around you in others?

What actions do you intend taking?

After writing the story of Malini Devi and Kate Spelling it was time for coffee and a break. I took the coffee outside and sat down on a bench outside the chalet. Looking out over the beach and the sea I realized that I was becoming refreshed. The break from work and the total absorption in writing had re-energised me and indeed enervated me in a way that I had not expected.

In that moment of relaxation I began to think of Michael Phillips and returned to my desk to write about him.

CHAPTER 13

Michael Phillips

It can be quite easy to be deflected or to lose interest in a detailed project that takes a great while to plan and execute. It takes patience and determination and a belief in the outcome for the plan to succeed. This is why many strategies can fall by the wayside because so many people do not have the grit and determination to see through what has been started.

A few years after I joined the company, an internal advertisement was placed inviting people to apply for positions to support the introduction of a Leadership Academy. This was a new venture for us and sounded very exciting. It involved the creation of Assessment Centres and the tests involved, the creation of a Leadership model, and the development of a curriculum (workshops, projects and job experiences) to be introduced over a few years. It also covered sourcing people to be included in the Academy both internally and externally.

The Board had reviewed the concept and accepted the idea that we needed to focus on creating a group of highly intelligent, experienced group of young managers who could progress to the highest levels in the company. Access to the Academy was open to all. The CEO and the Board were taking this seriously. They were convinced that top level Directors were far better developed from within than resorting to external hires which might have variable success.

There was no capability within the company to develop this and so the Board decided to headhunt a Director who had wide experience in this practice. After a while an announcement was made that Michael Phillips was to be appointed Academy Director. Michael, a man in his mid 50s, was a well known figure in the profession and had often spoken at conferences on the subject of leadership and capability. He was a great acquisition for the company as he had extensive experience in designing and implementing Leadership Academies.

I was tempted to apply for a position on the design and implementation team but at the time I had aspirations to be included in the Academy and reasoned that it might not be quite so easy if I was part of the team. One of my colleagues, Olivia Sturgess, was interested and she applied and joined the team.

Although she left the section to join Michael's team we often met and it was obvious that she was energized and enthused by Michael's grasp of what needed to be done. I met him a few times in those early days myself at various meetings as his team gathered data on how a Leadership model should be constructed for the company and the competences that were most associated with success.

He always seemed relaxed at these meetings. Olivia said to me that he simply knew what he was doing and spent a lot of time coaching the team to acquire the knowledge. He sent them off to other companies with whom he had been connected also to benchmark and to understand how a mature Academy helps to raise performance and engagement in the company.

When the plan was ready it was detailed. The Board had made it clear they wanted a leading edge Academy that was able to attract the best available young talent from top level Business Schools around the World.

The CEO in those days was an impatient man wanting results to be very visible. When Michael presented to the Board with a plan the CEO indicated that he wanted to see the first intake of internal and external participants by October of the following year. This gave the team around 12 months to achieve the deadline.

When I saw Olivia shortly after that Board meeting she seemed a little worried. I asked her why.

“The timetable to implement is very tight, David,” she said to me. As well as completing the tests, we need to contact the right business schools and seek applications, place internal advertisments, train internal assessors, set up testing centres. The logistics are immense.”

“What did Michael Phillips say?” I asked her.

“Nothing affects him David,” she responded. “He took it with a smile. He just said it was a stretching deadline but we would do it. He said we would ‘build the road one mile at a time’ and not worry about the next section until we get to it.”

Every now and then, bulletins would appear giving us an update on what was taking place and I applied of course when it was advertised internally. Olivia was hard to catch most of the time as the team worked long hours ‘building one mile of road at a time’.

She was involved a lot as an administrator at the testing centres over that period travelling to schools in Europe and a few in America. In June of that year I met her when she just returned from New York. We went out together one evening for a drink and I could sense that she was agitated. After a while I asked her what was troubling her.

She hesitated and looked at me as if she was searching for my ability to keep a confidence. “Olivia!” I protested. “You have known me for a long time. I have never betrayed a confidence and never will.”

“How do you know I want to share one?” she asked somewhat curious.

“I just know you do. It’s obvious,” I responded.

She looked down for a moment. “I heard something that Michel Phillips said to the CEO. It was amazing David,” she blurted out.

I nodded waiting for her to continue.

"We were in New York assessing," Olivia said. "We always have a preparation room for the Assessors and I try to organize a room for Michael from which he can work. In New York it was a small room connected to the preparation room. Michael's door was open. I was the only one in the preparation room as all the assessors and administrators were occupied with testing."

She paused. "The phone rang and Michael put it on speaker. I don't know why. I heard the CEO's voice."

"Yes?" I prompted.

"It went something like this:

'Michael, where are you?'

'I'm in New York with the assessing team – as you know from the schedule.'

'Hmmm. It's a detailed process isn't it, Michael?" the CEO said impatiently.

'Yes it is. If it's undertaken professionally it takes a lot of planning and execution time as you know. I was quite clear about that when we first met.'

(Pause)

"You know I'm wondering, Michael, whether it's all really worth…..'

"Michael Phillips must have got to his feet because I could hear the desk and chair moving," Olivia said. "He then said this:".

'Well bless me! I never took you for one of those people who get midstream in a plan and then want to turn back. Now you have surprised me! You haven't got bored with all this have you?"

“It went quiet for a moment” Olivia said. “Then I heard the CEO laugh a little. It sounded like nervous laughter.”

‘No, No, No,’ the CEO said in a more conciliatory tone. ‘I mean with your time. It’s taking a lot of your time. That’s what I mean.’

“It wasn’t you know David,” Olivia said. “You could tell that he really meant the Academy project. But it wasn’t finished Michael continued and followed up with another comment to the CEO. He said…..”

‘I am so glad to hear that. I would hate to hear that we have no resolve for things in this company. And don’t worry about my time. Once I’ve shown this team what to do they can run it without me soon.’

‘Good, good. When you get back, come to see me and we’ll have a chat about it all.’

“The phone went dead then and Michael Phillips gave the biggest laugh I have ever heard from him.” Olivia said. “After a moment he came out of his office and saw me sat there working.”

“He paused for a moment. ‘You must have heard all that Olivia?’ he said to me.”

“I nodded and gave him a silly little girl smile. I felt so stupid,” Olivia said remembering the moment.

“Well, I will rely on your discretion,” he said to me. ‘Just know this: when something is right and has been agreed don’t let anyone stop you whoever they are. Follow it through to the end so you can say to yourself that you always finish what you have started.’

“He left the room then to see how things were going. Of course I haven’t breathed a word to anyone and you are the only one to whom I would share this. Please don’t say anything David.”

“Of course I won’t,” I said to Olivia.

Later and often I reflected on what good advice Michael had given. It is so easy to give up but Michael Phillips had courage and determination and I have always hoped that I have it too.

Principle 12: Persevere to the end in any enterprise begun

No strategy is easy and sometimes it can seem easy to stop and try something else. However, unless it is clear that the strategy is a disaster all leaders should be determined and remain focused on completing what has been started.

Principle 12: Persevere to the end in any enterprise begun

Exercise: How much perseverance do you show in all your endeavours at work? Do you relentlessly pursue a goal until it is completed or are you inclined to give in if you meet obstacles?

Review the current status and decide what actions you will take?

Shortly after I finished writing the case of Michael Phillips Diane called me on my mobile phone.

"I'm taking the afternoon off", she said as soon as I answered the phone.

"Again?" I questioned in total surprise.

"Yes, I'm jealous of all this free time you are having without me. I'll meet you at the Swan in an hour and then come back with you to the chalet. There are some things I can do there anyway while you are writing."

"That's really great. Thank you Diane," I responded enthusiastically.

"You're sure I won't disturb you?" she asked.

"No, no. Not at all," I replied. "Once I'm writing, you'll have to throw a brick at me to get a response.

She laughed and we reaffirmed to meet at the Swan. I set an alarm on my mobile for 45 minutes and hoped I could get a long way or even complete the next chapter of the book. I had decided to write about Stephen Weaver, a totally different character to Michael Phillips.

CHAPTER 14

Stephen Weaver

When you are in a position of authority as a manager or leader you have a degree of power over others. The position of authority and the power that goes with it demands that it be used with integrity. In some cases also people are attracted to the leader because of the power that they hold. In some cases, employees are fearful of the power that the leader holds over them and their continuing employment. This demands that the leader knows where the line is. It is true that leadership does involve an element of emotion to connect people to the task in hand or the goal.

The majority of leaders use this in a professional way but sometimes the line can be crossed. The thinking brought me to consider the case of Stephen Weaver. Stephen worked out of our London Headquarters as an Audit Manager. He led a small team that carried out audits at stores throughout the UK. I realized, in hindsight, that it was a perfect cover for him.

Stephen commenced his career at one of the London stores after completing his A levels. He progressively made his way through the grades and gravitated towards audit because on the surface he enjoyed visiting other cities and meeting a wide range of people. He also argued at interviews that audits allowed him to see a wide range of best practices and business methods which he was able to bring to the attention of senior management, if they were unaware, and it enabled him to prepare for a higher position himself.

He was a single man in his mid thirties living in a reasonable apartment in London and little was known about his personal life except that he was passionate about Arsenal Football Club. He had only a few friends at the office in London. This was nothing exceptional for someone in Audit. Often they preferred to eat and socialise together either fearful that they might let some information slip or perhaps left alone by some employees who felt that they might let something slip!

Always smartly dressed and with an assured bearing, Stephen was well respected at the London Office. Having become very experienced at the process of Audit he was adept at providing exceptionally helpful reports. His approach was not to carry out visits searching for wrongdoing but rather to make the assumption that error was often unintended with no malicious intent. He was also quick to publish details, with the permission of the store, of best practice which might be implemented elsewhere. This practice made him something of a hero at stores in the provinces. The local General Managers and Managers of stores welcomed him openly to their stores as a result.

He did not visit our Headquarters restaurant that much when he was at the London Office. He preferred to take lunch outside somewhere. If he was there it was always because he was putting himself under pressure to meet a deadline. If I saw him there I would sometimes sit with him. Usually, I discussed with him his future career development but he always laughed this off. He maintained that he needed to learn a great deal more before he was ready for moving to another Department. On speaking to his manager, I found the same reluctance to accept that he be developed elsewhere. It wasn't surprising Stephen's capability in Audit was such that his boss felt it was unlikely that he would ever get anyone as good.

I had often thought that we project our own ambitions on to others and that if someone was comfortable in their position and fully effective then why should we make a change?

Things may well have continued for some considerable time if it were not for the fact that I received an anonymous letter in my mail. It was typed and unsigned:

"I did not know who to write to. I had heard your name mentioned at the store. They said you are a good person who listens. I hope so. I can't talk to anyone about this at the store but I can't let it continue any longer. I don't want to be afraid of what might happen anymore. I read stuff about Stephen Weaver in the Newsletter but he's not who you think he is. He is bad, very bad.

I know you visit the stores sometimes and if you visit our store I will recognize you and speak to you about Stephen but I don't want to say anything yet."

I was shocked about this. I wondered if it was a hoax or someone jealous of Stephen in some way or wanting to cause trouble for him for personal reasons. During the following week I telephoned the General manager of the Store to let him know I would be visiting to discuss matter with him and that my stay would be for two or three days.

During the first day of the visit, one of the office staff stopped me in the Staff Restaurant to ask if she could meet me at Starbucks in the High Street at 6pm. I agreed to do so.

We met at the agreed time. She was a woman in her late twenties and of striking appearance, but her features were troubled with worry. Once pleasantries were over she went straight to her story.

"My name is Jill Cox," she said to me. "I've been here straight from school and I like the job. I'm a single mother and it's hard sometimes. I have made mistakes. Yes made mistakes but I'm not a thief or a criminal. You people in London think Stephen is a wonder but he is evil, so evil."

She paused. "He found a financial error in my cash when he did the audit. He knew I'd borrowed it and I expected him to report me but he didn't. If he had I would have lost this job I know, but to be honest now I don't care."

She paused and hesitated again. "He replaced the missing money himself and said that it would be a secret between us because he had seen me at work and he really liked me. He said I had a future and this silly incident shouldn't stop me from progressing in the company. I couldn't believe it at first that he would cover it up for me. I thought he was an angel...... but then it started."

"What started?" I asked.

"Come on," she spat quickly and the restrained herself. "Think about it. He had me trapped. He works on you slowly with smile and chatting as if you are a special friend. Then he moves to asking you for coffee. He's slow about it like he gets fun from it. Each visit he takes a step further and when he comes next...well you know what I mean."

"It's only an allegation you know," I said to her.

She took an envelope from her bag. I recorded this when he was here last time. You will see. I nodded.

"Why are you telling me now?" I asked.

"I'm moving on," she said. "I didn't have a good experience in my first marriage but I've been dating a really nice guy for a while. We will marry soon and he's got a job in Dubai. We will leave in a month and I never want to see that horrible Stephen Weaver again."

I nodded.

"Please don't stop me will you," she pleaded. "I know I did wrong but Stephen he is using it. It's not right. If I told my guy.......Well....."

"Thanks," I said to her. "Don't Worry."

I left the store after a day or so and returned to my office in London. Jill Cox had given me much to think about. The envelope she sent me contained the recording of a conversation between them. It was clearly Stephen's voice and the intent was obvious.

Over the next couple of months I visited a number of Stores to make indirect enquiries. It was clear that Stephen had repeated his enterprise in several places. Some had willingly entered into the arrangement because they genuinely liked Stephen and thought he was helping them. Others had a haunted look that they were about to be found out.

By the time my investigation was complete I had a good dossier of evidence to discuss with Stephen. I discussed the case with the CEO and Stephen's direct boss in confidence.

"What's your advice?" The CEO asked.

"I'll suspend him while we carry out further investigations but the evidence seems quite clear. I'll see him today as he is at the office here."

He and Stephen's boss gave their assent.

When I called for Stephen to visit my office he was prepared. One of the girls who had been duped by his charm had obviously tipped him off. He gave me a letter of resignation as soon as he sat down.

"I'm sure you will want me to leave today," He said. "I cleared most of my things yesterday just a small bag in my office now. You can get security to check it if you like."

"What you did was despicable, Stephen," I said to him.

"I don't know what you have but I'm sure its all lies," he said to me. "Take me to court if you feel you have a case but I don't think so. In Audit there's a lot of people who have it in for you. My conscience is clear."

He got up to leave. "I bet it was that Jill Cox who told lies about me," he said. "When she cleared off to Dubai I guessed what was up. I tried to help her development of course but she had other ideas that I could not possibly entertain."

He winked at me and left the office.

Principle 13: Respect the dignity of others and do not abuse position

The exercise of power is a privilege. Leaders should never use their power to obtain favours from subordinates or others for any reason whatsoever. The dignity of juniors should always be maintained.

Principle 13: Respect the dignity of others and do not abuse position

The exercise of power is a privilege. Leaders should never use their power to obtain favours from subordinates or others for any reason whatsoever. The dignity of juniors should always be maintained.

Exercise: As you examine your conscience do you feel that any of your behaviours may be a subtle use of your power to take advantage of others? Do you see any of your peers or superiors using their power in an unfair way?

What actions can you take that will improve your performance and how can you influence others to behave in a way which is more professional?

The story of Stephen Weaver left a bad taste in my mouth and I felt myself clattering the keys on my laptop as it came to completion and indeed a few minutes later the alarm sounded on my mobile to remind me of my lunch with Diane.

Stephen's was indeed an awful story and so much in contrast to the character of Michael Phillips. I closed the laptop, locked up the chalet and drove over to the Swan.

It was so good to see Diane during the working week when there is no obligation to work! As I had thought so many times, Diane was not only my wife but my best friend whose company I wanted above all others. We probably lunched longer than intended but it was fun and we chatted and laughed for a considerable time. Eventually, when it was time to leave, a memory came to her.

"I forgot to tell you," she announced. "I was thinking we should invite Ed to stay soon. We haven't seen him for a while and he's back from an overseas mission now."

"What a great idea," I responded. It was true; we had not seen my brother for quite a while.

As we drove back to the chalet, thinking of my brother led on to thoughts of Colin Eggerton.

CHAPTER 15

Colin Eggerton

I attended a Conference in Manchester a few years ago. I am not necessarily a good networker – I should be better – but will always introduce myself to those I sit next to at the various sessions. In this case, I sat next to a man in his sixties who was well dressed – unlike myself – and who had the air of one with a distinguished career. We exchanged pleasantries and names. His name is Colin Eggerton and I established that he was retired and living in Cornwall close to Penzance.

The session that I had joined was one dealing with leadership and the importance of courage and standing your corner in an argument. It was an interesting discussion but I sensed that the basis of the argument was more about persistence and determination rather than courage.

After the presentation had concluded, I asked Colin what he thought about the presentation and he said he felt that courage can only emerge when you are afraid. That it was not something that you can talk about unless you have experienced real fear. I was curious about his comment and I suggested we talk further over lunch.

He did not wish to take lunch at the conference cafeteria and so we adjourned to a nearby hotel restaurant. I asked him to tell me about his career before we got down to the detail.

I was not that surprised when he informed me that he had commenced his career at Sandhurst and become an Army Officer, retiring as a Colonel. There was something about his step that had a military bearing. He informed me that he could talk of many acts of courage from officers and men when under fire but in those arenas he believed that courage was largely a desire "not to let your unit or your mate down". People would do things to help others because of the camaraderie formed in the unit.

"Courage in the Army is something you learn over time through the various actions you are involved in", he said and it's not often a requirement in civilian life. He maintained that in the Army, courage was part of the job and as such you did not really think about it.

But something he said afterwards encouraged me to think more deeply. He said that courage and honour were closely linked and that if you were dishonoured, then no matter how fearful you were, you needed to make a stand.

I was curious.

"Did something happen in the Army that makes you say this?" I asked

He laughed. "No, no" he responded. "It was after my Army career in the more political arena of the charity for which I worked for quite a few years."

"May I ask you what happened," I inquired.

"Yes, you might find it an ethical dilemma for you to conjure with," he replied.

"I'm curious," I responded. "Please go on."

"It was quite some years ago that I left the Army. I believed the skills I gained in the latter part of my career equipped for me an HR Director role," he stated. "I studied for and gained a Masters degree in Human Resources and also obtained full Membership of the Chartered Institute of Personnel and Development."

He continued. "A charity, I discovered, can be a very political organization but I guess I should not have been surprised. The Head of Legal was opposed to my appointment I discovered from the CEO. He wanted the CEO to hire someone that was known to him. The CEO informed me confidentially that he wanted a strong, independent person in the HR position who had no ties or allegiances with anyone in the company."

"Wise move," I said.

"From the first day of my arrival, the thinly veiled contempt was apparent. It was quite obvious that he despised entrants from the Army into senior positions in organisations," he stated. "At virtually every meeting where I was proposing changes to our HR strategy he made reference to the fact that military adaptations were unlikely to work in civilian life. Of course, all my proposals were designed for the not for profit sector and specifically for this charity. There was no association at all with anything military in any of my proposals."

"Did you find yourself getting angry?" I asked.

Colin laughed softly. "Not really," he said. "I found it amusing to a certain extent. When someone is insulting you the degree of anger you feel is, I think, connected to their inherent power and their ability to hurt or damage. I am somewhat older than you and a now long gone Labour politician, Dennis Healey, described a verbal attack from a political rival, Geoffrey Howe as akin to 'being savaged by a dead sheep.' It felt a little like that."

"Nevertheless……." I interjected.

"Yes, I know," he continued. "It's not something you can tolerate from a peer."

"Did the CEO do anything?" I asked.

"To be frank I asked him to do nothing," He responded. "It would appear I was clinging to 'mothers apron strings'. I have always stood up for myself."

I waited for him to continue.

"You are going to be challenged by someone at some time in your career whatever the organization. You have to face that challenge if you have done nothing wrong. In this case I had done nothing wrong and did not intend to let the veiled insults continue. However, the situation deteriorated rapidly."

He paused and continued. "Firstly, he wrote to a Country Director giving guidance and to a certain extent instruction on an HR matter. The Country Director sent it to me seeking clarification that it was approved by me. Then in an open meeting of Directors he raised a point unilaterally that I had failed in my role since my appointment and that I was damaging all professionals in the Charity with my incompetence."

I was shocked. "How could he say that without citing serious evidence?" I asked.

"Well, of course, he used some minor examples but the whole matter was shut down quickly by the CEO who asked that we both visit him in his office the following morning," he responded.

He laughed again. "It is strange when those around you think you are about to fall. They keep a distance as if the 'falling tower' might in some way cast debris and dust on them. I had no intention of falling of course."

"What did you do?" I asked.

"I visited his office late on in the afternoon. Most people had left the Charity Offices at that time," he responded. "He stiffened when he saw me enter his office. I think he thought I was going to 'call him out' and challenge him to a duel or just hit him!" he laughed. "Our exchange went something like this:"

"What do you want?" he said somewhat nervously to me, his eyes glancing behind me towards the door.

"Don't worry," I said to him. "Perhaps in the 18th century we would have taken to swords but I have come here to request that you apologise to the CEO for your behavior and then publicly at next week's Senior Management Team meeting."

"I'll think about it," he said and of course he was relaxing now that he felt no personal threat. "Is that all?" he said gesturing to the door and signaling my dismissal.

I sat down and put a file in front of him. "Take a look when I have left," I said to him. "In the first case you will apologise to the Country Director for accidentally stepping into my work area. In the second case your legal advice in the case of depositing money in certain accounts amounts to illegal tax sheltering. You will lead the Charity into difficulties with HMRC. I suggest you correct it quickly."

"I left at that point as I knew he was eager to examine the second document in the file."

"He called me on my mobile later that evening but I did not answer. We met at the CEO's office the following morning. The CEO spoke about teamwork and harmonious relationship and asked the Head of Legal to explain himself."

"The Head of Legal was naturally subdued. He apologized to the CEO and to me for his outburst and pleaded distressing domestic difficulties that had affected his organizational life. He also raised to the CEO that information which had been provided by me had made him realize that his recommendations for the placement of monies was potentially risky and accordingly the strategy would be rewritten. He thanked me for my advice." He continued.

"The CEO was taken aback but pleased at the outcome. He looked at me in surprise but I merely said that it had all been a misunderstanding between us," he stated. "At the next meeting he made a public apology for his outburst at the previous meeting."

"How did you know….?" I started to ask.

"About his error – deliberate or otherwise?" He asked and continued. "Arrogant people usually make autocratic decisions and rarely seek advice on their judgements. We all make mistakes but the arrogant more than most. If you are under unnecessary attack from someone you merely place in front of them the magnitude of their own error. It will always be there and you will always find it. There is no need to be aggressively confrontational but just stand your own ground and meet the challenge head on. I could have taken it to the CEO of course. But by giving it to him, I allowed him to correct the error."

"What about the relationship afterwards? I asked.

"Well I can't exactly say that we were bosom buddies but he gave me a grudging respect for the way the events played out. There were no further incidents."

Principle 14: Never backdown when an unfair challenge is made by a peer

Regrettably competition can find its way into peer to peer relations as some strive for recognition from the senior management team and to assume a position of superiority over their peers. This can take the form of an attack on others but leaders should never back away or cowed from an aggressive and unfair challenge from a peer.

Principle 14: Never backdown when an unfair challenge is made by a peer

Regrettably competition can find its way into peer to peer relations as some strive for recognition from the senior management team and to assume a position of superiority over their peers. This can take the form of an attack on others but leaders should never back away or cowed from an aggressive and unfair challenge from a peer.

Exercise: In examining the relationship with your peers do you detect any competition in your behaviour which is leading you to act in an unfair and unreasonable way?

Do you sense that such behaviour is being used against you?

Have you created a map of your peer relations which indicates positive, negative and neutral positions? If not create one and consider its relevance to your current postion and ability to achieve goals.

What actions will you take to remedy the situation?

I sat back in the chair after finishing the story about Colin and in a way he did remind me of my brother. It would not have surprised me if my brother were to act in a similar manner.

"I made some tea," Diane called out. "I sensed you may be reaching the end of that chapter."

I turned to her and smiled. "It won't be long and I will have finished this book, you know."

"Not bad for a week's work," she laughed. "Maybe you should go into this full time!"

"Now there's a thought," I responded reflecting on the idea. I looked out of the window. "Anyway, enough for today. Let's finish the tea and set off home."

As usual, once Diane and the children left, I got up to shower and breakfast and left for the chalet. I knew that this would be my last day of writing on this theme and once completed I could get back to work.

At my desk, I hesitated above the keys wondering which idea would emerge to cover the next principle. It came with remembering the story of Lily Stewart

CHAPTER 16

Lily Stewart

When we hire graduates we tend to hire those from very good Universities with proven levels of intelligence. We have found that two tests give us an indication of the level of intelligence for which we are searching. This is a verbal understanding test and numerical reasoning. In a way they both demand the ability to analyse and solve problems. We use a range of other tests of course but people rarely do well at the others if scores are below average in these two.

However, the tests are just one aspect of our assessment. The ability to analyse and solve problems is a great asset to an organization but these are nothing unless an individual possesses the qualities of determination, persistence and resilience. We have always wanted people who will not give up; if they are knocked down they will get up quickly and continue the fight. A straightforward interview or series of interviews rarely gives an indication of this but an extended assessment centre will do so. The number of tests and the type of test always varies in difficulty and focuses on analysis and decision making individually and in groups and under time pressure. As well as tests, however, the candidates experience two one hour interviews with one assessor who examines problem solving capability and another who assesses motivational behavior. The third interviewer is the Assessor Chair who discusses the tests with the candidate more than anything else and their enjoyment of the experience – or not.

We know that the intelligence is a given and those who do not have the stomach for a tough experience may well not turn up on the day. Others may well not return after breaks or decide not to continue into the second day. We do not mind this because what we are looking for is "staying power" and that ability never to give in is often the difference between project success and failure, organizational success and failure.

There are many signals and observation opportunities at Assessment Centres that a skilled assessor will register regarding a potential new hire. Not only is it the fact that they turn up and are on time! There are other signals. What is the interaction between the potential new hires as they are in the waiting area? Do they show one face to the assessors and another to their peers? How do they behave towards the administrators ? Do they leave the premises at breaks and lunchtime or network and socialize with the others?

We design the layout of the Assessment Centres so that the Assessors and Adminstrators Common room are stationed at the rear of the Centre. This means that the Assessors and Administrators are obliged to pass through waiting areas and dining areas as well as pass test rooms and interview rooms quite regularly. This gives an opportunity to observe candidate behavior as they move about.

Lily Stewart attended one of our Assessment Centres in London. I tend to wait with the administrators as candidates arrive and are issued their badges, timetable and other information. Lily was one of the first to arrive and it was clear that she was a little anxious. She took some water and found herself a seat to await the commencement of the activities. As others arrived and took seats I noticed some hesitation within her but eventually she left her seat and joined some of the other candidates. She listened more than spoke and occasionally asked questions.

Our Assessment Centres begin with a gathering of the candidates. We try to arrange groups of twenty four which we can subdivide into groups of six when we are running group exercises.

At the commencement of the Centre a briefing takes place in a hall or auditorium. The assessors and administrators are lined up. The Assessor Chair runs through the timetable and advises candidates to eat well during the days of the assessment and to get a good night sleep after the first day. We know from experience that the first day is tiring. They are also informed that the success rate is normally 1 in 8.

Of all the 24 on that day it was Lily who appeared the most resolute but as the opening remarks progressed her face turned pale at the difficulties which would lay ahead. As I walked through the common areas of the Assessment Centre those two days I saw Lily on occasions. Sometimes she sat alone and occasionally I saw her reassuring candidates who assumed they might not have performed well on a particular test.

I did not take part in any of the tests that day or in the group exercises as it was more common for me to have the position of Assessor Centre Chair. In this role the Chair moderates the results from the assessors and seeks evidence to defend a decision to accept or not. A simple rating system is used :

1 – IP : Immediate Pass

2 – QP: Qualified Pass – may be a full pass once assesses against the performance of others

3 B : Borderline

4 NS: Not Suitable

The two Assessors' ratings for Lily were Borderline. She had exceptional scores on the Number and Verbal Test and on the In Tray Exercise. She also scored well in both her interviews with the Assessors but the problem seemed to lie in her presentation and her participation in a Group Exercise. Despite her attempts, robust participants seemed to have shouldered her out of the Group Exercise and her voice was not heard. Also she seemed to stammer her way through the presentation even though the logic of her argument was very good.

In some rare circumstances we reviewed cases like this and I asked the assessors if they had any objection if we did. Neither disagreed. I had seen her briefly at her Chair Interview and been impressed with her intelligence and her problem solving capability. In agreement with the Assessors I asked that she present to the three of us on this occasion. I met her to discuss this.

"Why are you doing that?" she asked me. "Haven't you – or rather your assessors - already seen it?"

"I'll be very frank with you," I said to her. "You have done well on most of the tests with the exception of your presentation and at the Group Exercise."

She sighed. "Yes I thought so," she paused and looked away for a moment. "I lack confidence in giving presentations and I am a little shy with others. I am twenty-one now and I had hoped that I would have found a way to combat it by now but I have not."

"Will you give the presentation to us again?" I asked.

"Yes I can of course if you wish. I will try to do better this time," she said resolutely.

Shortly afterwards we met her in the meeting room where she was waiting to deliver her presentation. It was clear that she was nervous but also there was grit and determination in her face.

"Would you please take us through your presentation?" I asked her.

She nodded and took a deep breath. It was true that the content of her presentation was very good but nerves seemed to get the better of her during the delivery. She stammered on occasions and her voice broke and occasionally it was evident that she was annoyed with herself.

I had pre-arranged that the three of us would applaud on completion of her presentation and she looked at us in surprise at the end, unsure at first if she was not being mocked.

My co-assessors left at the end of the presentation and I asked her questions to challenge her assumptions. She answered them fluently and with confidence. She demonstrated excellent insights into the problem and initiative in how she would solve the problem.

I thanked her when it was completed and I waited.

"I won't ever give up you know," she said to me.

"Give up on what?" I asked.

"On being a manager or maybe a leader. I won't ever give up." She said with resolution. "It is hard for me to participate in a selection process like this but I would go through it a thousand times to get the opportunity to achieve my ambition."

"Even though you find it so difficult?" I asked her.

"Even so." she said firmly. "I know I will get past it. In my mind's eye I can vision a future me who will speak fluently and influentially. It will come."

"You are right, it will," I responded. "With practice and training you can get past this."

We went on to discuss other matters and afterwards I recalled the two Assessors. The Chair of the Assessment Centre had a right to pass a candidate if he or she believed that there was good reason to do so despite the Assessor ranking. This never happens for someone who is classed as Not Suitable, but occasionally a Borderline candidate may receive a Pass. I discussed it in depth with the Assessors who, after discussion, had no objection to her inclusion.

The selection proved to be worthwhile. Lily went on to become a very good speaker with a charismatic and influential style and became a very good leader of people with a track record of achievement. She was selected that day not because of her intelligence and incisive thinking but because she refused to give up. She was the type never to give up and that is a quality that leaders need to show all the time. When speaking at Harrow in 1941 Winston Churchill made the words famous in his "Never, ever, ever, ever give up" speech.

Principle 15: A good leader always shows courage and determination in the face of difficulty

Courage is an essential feature of leadership. A lack of it may often mean that individuals will choose a weaker course of action which will not benefit the organization or company.

Principle 15: A good leader always shows courage and determination in the face of difficulty

Courage and determination are essential features of Leadership. A lack of them may often mean that individuals will choose a weaker course of action which will not benefit the organization or company.

Exercise: Consider difficult situations you are facing and honestly assess if you are avoiding the correct course of action. Do you see any complacency or lack of determination in your team?

How will you build a sense of urgency and determination in yourself and others to achieve higher performance?

Once the chapter of Lily was complete, I stopped and made coffee. I sat outside on the bench to think for a while as I was now coming to the story which had originated the idea of the book. This story was now about me and whilst drinking the coffee I shaped it in my mind and then returned to write it.

CHAPTER 17

David Adams

It was a routine assignment in a sense for me although perhaps not for those involved. Over the years I led a number of reorganisations leading to job reassignment and in somes cases early retirement or redundancy. My personal experience was that if you handled the matter with empathy and listened to what people really wanted, then the assignment could be handled well and without unnecessary conflict.

In this particular case, I was asked to look at and rationalize the number of stores in line with economic changes in various locations and handle the consequential human resources issues.

My prior experience taught me to communicate quickly in these cases and to keep communicating. Unions were well informed and likewise all staff. I set up a number of "surgeries" on a regular basis to keep people informed. Everyone was issued with a personal letter asking them to state their choices of job, location, voluntary redundancy etc. In addition, where consolidation led to new and higher graded positions these were advertised so that interested employees might apply.

On this occasion, I led the team and one of my peers from Operations, Danny Aitken, worked with me. Danny had excellent knowledge of operations and logistics on the ground and his input was vital in terms of ensuring success of the reorganization.

There had always been a friendly rivalry between us as we progressed our careers, but this never stopped us from enjoying good dinners together when we were travelling and sharing information.

This reorganization we worked on together was relatively trouble free and we reassigned and redeployed virtually all employees without problem except for one problem that took me totally by surprise.

There were two candidates for the position of Customer Services Manager. The one was a man of thirty five who I had met before but did not know well and the other was a single woman of around thirty years of age. She had not worked for me but for a couple of years we worked together in close proximity in London after she was recruited. She had a reputation for quality work. This Customer Service Manager position was the only one that created serious contention for the position.

We interviewed both candidates and provided them with an opportunity to make a presentation asking each to give us a plan for what they would do if they were appointed to the position. Given the fact that I knew of the female candidate I requested the participation of Danny and another Manager in the selection process.

There was an arrogance about the male candidate as if the job was already his and his presentation was ill thought through and gave the impression that it had been rushed. It was standard customer service thinking and showed little innovation or original thinking.

The female candidate however, had researched extensively and looked at customer service techniques and practices in the hotel industry and airlines and made a pitch for some of the practices to be adapted to our industry. Additionally, she was alive to the use of advanced technology to improve customer service.

It was the unanimous conclusion of the selection team that the position should be offered to the female candidate. The male manager was placed in an equivalent position but not in customer service. We all agreed that he did not necessarily have the interpersonal skills for the role. And so with all the human resource and operational issues resolved satisfactorily our team disbanded and we returned to our usual roles.

A couple of weeks later the Chairman asked me to visit him in his office. This was not unusual as we conferred regularly on various issues. The initial stages of the meeting were as normal but I could sense that the Chairman was uncomfortable about something. The reason became clear when there was a pause in the conversation and the Chairman said, "I need you to look at this, David. Tell me what you think about it."

He handed over a folded paper to me. I opened it up to read the following. It was addressed to the Chairman.

"Please forgive me for writing to you directly and for not following normal grievance procedure channels. I am writing to you as Mr. David Adams works closely with you and feel that you should know something about the circumstances.

Recently, I was interviewed by Mr Adams, Mr Aitken and another manager for a position of Customer Service Manager in my Region. Given my background, experience, length of service and skills, I expected that the appointment would be a formality. However, a junior female candidate with less seniority and experience was given the position.

Normally, I would accept such a decision as this but I believe that Mr. Adams' personal involvement with the female candidate led to his favouring her appointment and influencing the other panel members accordingly.

It is well known that when she arrived in London that Mr. Adams commenced an affaire with her and her subsequent appointment to this Region was because of his influence. I am not saying that he maintained this relationship over a period of time but he certainly renewed it when he came here to head up the reorganization.

He was seen on several occasions with her at a hotel that was not the hotel where he was staying. On one occasion he did not return to his own hotel.

I believe that he recommenced a personal relationship with her and that this relationship led to her being appointed as Customer Services Manager.

This being so, I wish to submit a grievance to you and for this matter to be investigated."

I handed the paper back to the Chairman and looked at him pointedly for a moment. "Do you believe it?" I asked him.

"Of course not, David," He responded promptly. "I have known you for years and know your ethics. But I have to tell you something."

He had paused. "Yes?" I questioned asking him to continue.

"Danny Aitken said that he saw you with her one evening as he was passing the hotel," the Chairman stated.

"You showed him this?" I questioned, feeling an irritation beginning to arise. "So you believe it!"

"No of course not, David," The chairman responded quickly.

"Then, may I ask how he came to say this if he has not seen the grievance?" I asked.

"Look, I know that there has been a rivalry between you and Danny for years. I am aware of it, of course." The Chairman stated. He continued. "He may have heard a rumour, that you obviously have not, that we are considering you for a major advancement."

"I had heard something of the kind but I ignore these things," I responded.

"Well, alright," he continued. "While discussing the success of the reorganisation with Danny, he mentioned in passing to me that he had seen you with her. Of course he said that there was probably nothing in it."

I laughed out loud. "You should carry out an investigation," I said. "An allegation has been made and you cannot ignore it, especially if a peer is hinting at something. I tell you what I will do. I have a lot of leave not taken so I will take a week or two off as now if you have no objection. I can come in to answer any questions once you need me but I think I should be away from the office for now."

"Some might think your absence could be associated with guilt," he said.

"Chairman, it doesn't really matter to me what people think. It only matters what is true and I know the truth. And there is nothing in this as your investigation will show. Anyway, I need a break and it's time for me to do some thinking.

He thought about it and nodded his assent reluctantly.

It was at this point that I decided to let Diane know why I had decided to take some time off to write. My leave was almost up and my meeting with the Chairman was scheduled for the coming Monday. I called her from the chalet.

"I've almost finished the last principle in this book"," David said to her "it's an important one as it features me."

"Features you?" Diane said in mild surprise. "Why is that?"

"I didn't tell you before but actually I'm under investigation and I decided to take some time off and the idea of this book formed." Diane didn't speak so I continued. "A manager submitted a grievance claiming that I favoured a female member of staff and gave her a position because I was in an in appropriate relationship with her."

She stared at me for a while and then smiled. "You think I didn't know about this. Of course I was aware of what was happening. I just decided to wait for you to decide when it was the right moment to open the subject."

Of course, I reflected. My sudden absence would not have gone unnoticed at work. The grapevine would have been buzzing.

"They will declare that there is no case to answer on Monday. You know that, don't you Diane?" I asked her.

"Of course," she responded with absolute sincerity. "I've known you for so long, David. I just wonder if you should not have revealed the truth to the Chairman before you decided to do this."

This made me stop to think as my wife, as usual, had made a strong point. If I had informed him then one or two phone calls would have confirmed the truth.

"You have a point. Maybe I should have." I responded. "Anyway, at least I got to write this book."

"Yes, I'm proud of you in doing that. Now let's get you back to work, clear this up and get your career back on track," she said.

"Yes let's do that but I think I will continue to write also.

I returned to work on Monday and met with the Chairman.

"The allegation is without foundation of course," He said perhaps with a hint of relief, I thought. "But why didn't you tell me at our first meeting that the woman you were meeting was your sister?"

"Maybe I should have done so, but at the time I thought it would have looked like a protest. I could have said something to the team at the time but my sister was going through some personal difficulties and I did not really wish to air this also. For sure they would have wondered why she was visiting me. Unfortunately, her hair colouring and style is similar to the female candidate," I said to him. "In any event it was good that the investigation proved that at no time was I in contact, outside of an official capacity, with any of the employees in the Region."

"Yes, it's irritating that someone can make an allegation to tarnish the reputation of a good person but it seems that this was the case here," the Chairman said. "I am assured he will send you a letter of apology and a full retraction."

"He probably would not have made those allegations if someone had not prompted him to do so," I stated.

"What do you mean?" He asked and I sensed I had opened up a channel which should have remained closed.

"It doesn't matter now but my instincts tell me he was urged to do so. However, I have enjoyed my leave and now I'm glad to be back at work," I said to him.

The Chairman thought about it but chose not to inquire further about my statement and I was happy that this was so.

Nevertheless, I believed that I had behaved badly in this case. I was reasonably sure that Danny Aiken had put a game in play to undermine my possible progression. Instead of telling the truth about the situation I participated in the game and I regretted this.

Principle 16 – A leader always tells the truth without evasion

The truth about a situation is the only way for a leader to speak and behave. Any other route- other than transparency - is not the principle of a Leader and creates further complexities at a later stage.

Principle 16 – A leader always tells the truth without evasion

The truth about a situation is the only way for a leader to speak and behave. Any other route – other than transparency - is not the principle of a leader and creates further complexities at a later stage.

Exercise: Ask yourself the question if you are truthful and transparent in all things at work? If not what actions will you take to ensure this is so?

What will you do to ensure your team behaves in similar fashion?

AFTERWORD

Contemplation

It is interesting to note that Medieval Knights carried out a 10 hour long vigil before their Knighthood Ceremony. During the vigil the Knight would deeply contemplate the enormity of the responsibilities he would take up on becoming a Knight and pledging, amongst other things, to defend others.

In similar terms, when individuals are placed in charge of people in a company or organization they too now have a duty of care for others. There is, however, no contemplation on the enormity of this responsibility and many people become supervisors and managers of people without understanding how they should use the power that they have now been given.

It is well understood how a toxic manager may affect the life and well being of those whom they supervise, but in reality little is done to change it. For a knight to break a vow in medieval times the consequences were severe and he was likely to experience guilt and a deep sense of shame as he was literally outcast by his peers.

Toxicity

Without a code and without a sense of feeling guilt and shame we will continue to allow bad managers and leaders to continue to ply their destructive trade. In many cases the tangible results they produce in terms of business outcomes may be the reason that their personal behaviour is ignored.

It is a well-worn phrase that "people don't leave companies they leave managers". And in most cases this is probably true. Breaking any one of the principles we have seen in this book can lead to the early departure of great people who add value.

Adherence to these principles will reduce the likelihood of good people leaving.

We must not forget also that toxic managers can induce early "burnout" of their subordinates through their behaviours and this often goes unnoticed.

Similarly, although there are many rules and regulations to deal with harassment it still exists in bullying, intimidation and in the area of sexual harassment. Truly noble and honourable leaders would not engage in these activities.

But we have to change that. We want people to adhere to these principles, Find Nobility and practise it.

This is because work itself is ennobling and enriching. Leaders who do have honour and nobility use their core Leadership principles to enthuse others through their integrity, their ability to deal with change, their capacity to engage others and through their voice which inspires others to connect to the organization mission and values.

These leaders know that what people want from their work is:

- Some freedom to carry out their tasks in the way they want to
- The opportunity to learn and gain mastery
- To find meaning in what they do and know that it matters
- To enjoy a team spirit or relatedness within their work group

Great leaders know this! Great leaders know how to help people become the best that they can be.

Great leaders have honour and nobility and that is why they are followed. And it can be achieved by you also.

So what can You do?

In the final drafting of this book I came across a piece in the January-February 2016 edition of the Harvard Business Review with Professor Sreedhari Desai of UNC's Kenan-Flagler Business School. The basis of the piece was "Can you really insulate yourself from wrongdoing by advertising your values. Or will people think you are being 'holier than thou'".

It does not matter what level of manager you may be there is a probability that at some stage you may be called upon to carry out something which is unethical. This is a horrible moment. However, the essence of Professor Desai's work is this: If the person who is going to ask you to do this perceives you as a person who is morally 'pure' they will feel that asking you to get 'dirty' makes an ethical transgression even worse. Or the asker may be concerned that you will simply refuse.

Where quotations dealing with honour and integrity are displayed or symbols of honour Professor Desai discovered that people were less likely to be asked to do something "shady."

It is true that some cultures may be skeptical of people declaring for integrity, honour and principle and indeed may even be suspicious of motives. Nevertheless, this is a price worth paying.

There are many symbols for honour and integrity but the one that will be associated with this work is that of an elk, an anvil, a blue shield and an angel. They all depict strength and fortitude as well as honour.

Wearing one of these will indicate your willingness to follow the right path and the choice of which icon is entirely personal. The icon symbols I have selected are below.

Final Words

It is not easy to follow a path of nobility, honour and principle but in doing so you create a culture of integrity that others will respect and follow.

Maurice Collis

27 December 2016

www.ingramcontent.com/pod-product-compliance
Lightning Source LLC
Chambersburg PA
CBHW032023170526
45157CB00002B/835

* 9 7 8 1 4 8 3 4 8 4 1 6 7 *